Barrier-Free Travel
NATIONAL PARK LODGES
for Wheelers and Slow Walkers

Candy B. Harrington

PHOTOGRAPHS BY

CHARLES PANNELL

CANDY & CHARLES CREATIVE CONCEPTS

ISBN: 978-0-9985103-6-1

Candy & Charles Creative Concepts
PO Box 278
Ripon, CA 95366-0278

To Charles

Contents

Preface

Amazing Spaces in Spectacular Places

National park lodges are definitely amazing spaces. Granted they all have location going for them, but these majestic properties are much more than just chain hotels planted at precipitous points in our national lands. A great deal of thought went into their design and even their orientation.

Take Old Faithful Lodge in Yellowstone, and the Ahwahnee in Yosemite, for example. Both properties were designed by Gary Underwood, and although they both feature floor-to-ceiling windows, a massive lobby and the requisite oversized fireplace; they each also include individual design touches that truly makes them one-of-a-kind properties.

And as far as orientation goes, look no further than Far View Lodge in Mesa Verde National Park. The lodge was designed to reflect the solitude in the surrounding land; and the rooms face the adjacent mesa, and feature large picture windows and comfortable outdoor areas to enjoy the magnificent view.

National park lodges are more than just places to spend the night. They are places to extend your visit, enjoy the park after dark, and totally immerse yourself in the surrounding beauty. And each national park lodge is completely different.

And that's the main reason I wrote this book

The first national park lodge I ever visited was Camp Curry in Yosemite National Park. I was 13, and I was on a girlfriends skiing getaway with some of my besties and their families. Even though it was close to home it was still quite the treat for us. Snow covered the surrounding forest floor, and one night on our way back from the bathroom my pals and I had an impromptu moonlight snowball fight. And of course there was a lot of giggling — after all we were 13 — before an adult opened his cabin door and unceremoniously schussed us. And then we continued giggling — and pelting each other with snowballs — as we ran through the forest back to our cabin.

That's what memories are made of — these amazing spaces in spectacular places.

And over the years I've been privileged to spend some time in all the national park lodges; and indeed each one holds a very special memory for me.

The Grand Canyon Lodge North Rim is especially memorable, as I had an appointment to meet the manager there before the property opened up for the season. The place was completely deserted — it was just Charles, me and the deer. The manager showed up after we finished our picnic lunch, and when she took us into the main lodge building I had flashbacks of scenes from *The Shining*. It's amazing how creepy a deserted lodge can be, especially when it's so massive.

The Roosevelt Cabins in Yellowstone produced another memorable experience. We snuggled together in our cozy log cabin one night while the wind whipped up outside; and the next day we were treated to an up-close-and-personal bison encounter, just steps from our front door.

Finally, I'll never forget the night we spent at Rock Harbor Lodge in Isle Royale National Park. It absolutely poured down rain that night, so much so that it startled me from my sleep. We awoke the next morning to be greeted by a gorgeous sunrise, as the waves peacefully lapped at the lakeshore. From tempestuous to breathtaking in less than six hours — it was quite a ride.

And my hope is that these national park properties will create equally poignant memories for you too.

Now let's talk access, because, after all that's my expertise. That's another reason I wrote this book, to let folks know that these historic lodges are for the most part accessible. Granted, most were constructed before the Americans with Disabilities Act (ADA) was ever enacted, however access upgrades have been continually added over the years. Many people assume these lodges are not wheelchair-accessible, but that couldn't be further from the truth. So I've included detailed access descriptions and copious photos of the accessible rooms to prove this point.

Of course, lodgings are only part of the access equation. With that in mind I've also included an Access Overview section for each park, which lists some of the most accessible trails, attractions and access upgrades; and gives folks a good idea about the general accessibility of the parks. This book goes well beyond just stating that something is ADA compliant — it's a realistic assessment of the access so you can choose the parks that will work for you.

And if your time in a park is limited, be sure and read the Don't Miss This section, which includes the one absolutely must-do accessible trail, attraction or activity in the park. And again this is gleaned from first-hand experience, and a lot of legwork.

In the same vein, I've also included an Insider Tip section for each park, which is filled with helpful suggestions of things to look for, avoid or take into consideration when planning your visit. Your time is valuable, and I discovered most of these tips the hard way, so that you don't have to.

In the end, *Barrier-Free Travel; National Park Lodges for Wheelers and Slow Walkers* is the perfect tool to help you decide what parks and lodges will work best for you, and to plan an accessible national park road trip.

Additionally, access is constantly improving, so if you find something new, let me know, and I'll update things at www.BFNationalParkLodges.com.

So get out and explore our beautiful national parks, and then spend a night or two in the national park lodges listed in this book. And let me know how it goes. I'm sure it will be a memorable experience for you as well.

Candy Harrington

candy@EmergingHorizons.com
www.CandyHarrington.com
www.EmergingHorizons.com

Facebook: Candy Harrington
Twitter: Candy B. Harrington
Pinterest: Candy Harrington

Before You Go

Divided by state, this book contains 52 wheelchair-accessible national park lodges throughout the US mainland. Although each listing is accompanied by numerous photos and a detailed access description, it should be noted that not every property in this book will work for every wheelchair-user and slow walker. Everyone has different needs, so it's important to contact the property directly if you have additional access questions.

A general Access Overview section is also included with each park listing, which outlines the accessible sights, attractions and trails in each park. Some parks are more accessible than others, so again your choices will ultimately depend on your abilities. Additional resources for pre-trip research are listed at the end of each chapter. There are also more photos, tips and some accessible itineraries listed at www.BarrierFreeNationalParks.com.

Park Passes

Admission fees for the parks are listed at the beginning of each chapter. The National Park Service also offers a gaggle of money-saving passes.

Access Pass

This free lifetime pass provides for free admission to all national parks, and is available to U.S. citizens or residents with a permanent disability. Applicants must provide documentation of a permanent disability, and prove residency or citizenship. The pass also offers a 50% discount on campsites and boat launch fees. It generally does not provide for a discount on fees charged by concessionaires.

Military Pass

The free annual Military Pass provides for free park admission, and is available to active members of the Army, Navy, Air Force, Marines and Coast Guard. Reserve and National Guard Members are also eligible. A Common Access Card or Military ID (Form 1173) is required to obtain this pass.

Senior Pass

This lifetime pass provides free park admission, and is available to U.S. citizens or permanent residents age 62 or older. The cost of the pass is $80. An annual Senior Pass is also available for $20, and the cost for this annual pass can be applied to the purchase of a lifetime pass. Proof of age and residency or citizenship are required. The pass also offers a 50% discount on campsites and boat launch fees. It generally does not provide for a discount on fees charged by concessionaires.

Annual Pass

If you plan on visiting a number of national parks throughout the year, the Annual Pass may be a good deal for you. This non-transferable pass costs $80 and it's good for free park admission to all national parks for the entire year. It's an especially attractive deal if you live near a national park, or are planning a road trip that includes a number of national parks. You can also order this pass by calling (888) 275-8747.

Annual 4th Grade Pass

This free annual pass is available to all 4th graders and is valid for the duration of the 4th grade school year and the following summer. Paper vouchers can be obtained at www.everykidinapark.gov and exchanged for an Annual 4th Grade Pass at any national park entrance. This pass is also available to home-schooled students.

Authorized Park Concessionaires

All of the lodgings inside the national parks listed in this book are operated by authorized concessionaires, who have contracted with the National Park Service, and operate under strict guidelines. They are responsible for the daily operations of the facilities, as well as improvements and upgrades. It's important to deal with these concessionaires directly when you make a reservation; as not only will they give you the best prices, but you will also have access to employees that can block the accessible rooms and describe the access features of each available unit.

Unfortunately these concessionaires do not always come up first in internet searches because paid advertisements appear before them. Some of these paid advertisements even list "national park lodges" that are located many miles outside the parks, which is very misleading to people who are unfamiliar with the geography of the parks. The authorized concessionaires for all the national park properties are listed at the end of each chapter. Again, deal directly with these concessionaires for all lodging reservations.

Elevation

Although the symptoms of altitude sickness generally do not appear at elevations under 8,000 feet, wheelchair-users, slow walkers and people with compromised immune systems may feel the effects of increased altitudes at significantly lower elevations. Symptoms can include headaches, dizziness, shortness of breath, lethargy, insomnia and gastrointestinal disturbances. If you are unfamiliar with the effects that higher elevations have on your body, it's best to take it slow and drink plenty of water for the first few days at any increased elevation, especially if you live at sea level. Additionally, you may want to consult your doctor regarding the effects that increased elevations may have on your specific condition. To assist you in your travel planning, elevations are listed in the Access Overview section of each chapter.

Service Animals

In October 2018, the National Park Service (NPS) issued a new system-wide policy regarding the use of service animals by persons with disabilities in national parks. The revised policy aligns the NPS policy with the standards established by the Department of Justice (DOJ) and the Americans with Disabilities Act (ADA).

Under the policy, a service animal is defined as any dog that is individually trained to do work or perform tasks for the benefit of an individual with a disability, including a physical, sensory, psychiatric, intellectual, or other mental disability.

Service animals-in-training are not considered service animals.

Although the DOJ definition of a service animal only refers to a dog, the NPS must make reasonable modifications to policies, practices, or procedures to permit the use of a miniature horse by a person with a disability if the miniature horse has been individually trained to do work or perform tasks for the benefit of the individual with a disability.

The work or tasks performed by a service animal must be directly related to the individual's disability. Some examples of work or tasks performed may include:

- Assist individuals who are blind with navigation
- Alert individuals who are deaf to the presence of people or sounds
- Pull a wheelchair

- Alert individuals to the presence of allergens or the onset of a seizure
- Retrieve items
- Provide physical support and assistance to individuals with mobility disabilities
- Help individuals manage psychiatric and neurological disabilities

The crime deterrent effects of an animal's presence and the provision of emotional support, well-being, comfort, or companionship do not constitute work or tasks for the purposes of this definition.

Emotional support animals, therapy animals and companion animals are not recognized as service animals by the NPS.

All animals that are not classified as service animals are considered pets, and are subject to the pet regulations of the park, which can be found on the individual park websites. Service animals are allowed access to all areas of the park, including lodgings, restaurants, trails and attractions.

It should also be noted that although some organizations sell "service animal registration" documents on-line, these documents do not convey any rights under the ADA; and the DOJ and the NPS does not recognize them as proof that a dog is a service animal.

For more information on the ADA (and the NPS) definition of a service animal, visit www.ada.gov.

What is an Accessible Trail?

This book contains a number of trails that are rated as accessible by the National Park Service. It's important to understand that a trail does not have to be flat and paved in order to be accessible. The accessibility rules are laid out in the Architectural Barriers Act Accessibility Guidelines for Outdoor Developed Areas, that were published in the Federal Register on September 26, 2013. This rule became effective on November 25, 2013, for newly developed and substantially altered trails in federal outdoor developed areas.

This section is included to explain what you can expect to find on a trail that is rated as accessible in a federal area. It does not necessarily mean that you can access it, but rather that it follows the standards and regulations for an accessible trail. For this reason, even if a trail is rated as accessible, the access features of it will still be described in this book. Additionally, many trails that are not rated as accessible are included in this book, as they will work for many wheelchair-users and slow walkers.

Surface and Width

- Accessible trails must be firm and stable.

- There can be no openings, gaps or tread obstacles along an accessible trail.

- Accessible trails must be at least 36-inches wide.

Running Slope

- No more than 30% of the the total length of an accessible trail may have a running slope greater than 1:12 (8.33%). A 1:12 slope includes a one-foot rise ever 12 inches.

- Running slopes between 1:12 (8.33%) and 1:10 (10%) are allowed in 30-foot segments, with resting intervals at the top and bottom of each segment.

- The running slope of an accessible trail may never exceed 1:8 (12%).

Cross Slope

- The cross slope of accessible concrete, asphalt or wooden trails must not exceed 1:48 (2%).

- The cross slope of accessible trails constructed out of other materials must not exceed 1:20 (5%).

Scope

This does not mean that all federal trails developed or altered after the effective date of this regulation are required to be accessible. When conditions make it impracticable to construct an accessible trail, that trail may be exempt from the technical requirements. For example, Bright Angel Trail in Grand Canyon National Park, is not required to be accessible because it would be impracticable to construct one due to the steep terrain.

Arizona

The Rim Trail in Grand Canyon National Park

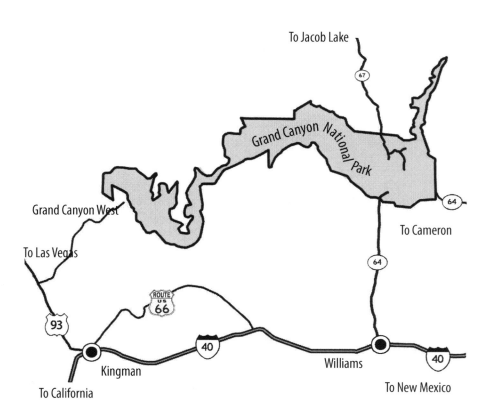

To Jacob Lake

67

Grand Canyon National Park

64

Grand Canyon West

To Cameron

To Las Vegas

64

93

ROUTE US 66

40

Williams

40

Kingman

To California

To New Mexico

Grand Canyon National Park

Located in Northern Arizona, the massive Grand Canyon measures 277 miles long, a mile deep and 18 miles across at its widest point. The national park covers about 1,900 square miles, and includes the popular South Rim and the more remote North Rim. And although the canyon itself is rather rugged, wheelchair-users and slow walkers can enjoy spectacular views from a copious collection of accessible trails and viewpoints that dot both rims. Even if you can't ambulate far, you'll still be treated to breathtaking canyon vistas from accessible overlooks that are just steps from the park lodges.

Grand Canyon National Park has three entrances — two for the South Rim and one for the North Rim. The South Entrance and the East Entrance both allow access to the South Rim. The South Entrance — which is the busiest entrance — is located on Highway 64 near Tusayan, about an hour from Williams. The East Entrance is at the far east end of Desert View Drive, about 30 miles west of Cameron, Utah. The North Entrance, which only allows access to the North Rim, is located 30 miles south of Jacob Lake on Highway 67.

The South Rim is open year-round; however some park roads may close following winter storms, until the snowplows can clear them. The North Rim is closed in the winter, as Highway 67 is not plowed. Most of the North Rim facilities are also closed from October 15 to May 15, so this area of the park has a limited season.

Grand Canyon National Park has six lodges, five of which are wheelchair-accessible. Five of these lodges are located on the South Rim and one is located on the North Rim.

Admission

$35 – seven-day pass
$70 – yearly pass

Spend the Night
El Tovar Hotel

1 El Tovar Road
Grand Canyon, AZ 86023
(888) 297-2757
www.grandcanyonlodges.com

The El Tovar Hotel dates back to 1905, making it the oldest property in the park. It's considered the premier lodging facility at the Grand Canyon, and it has hosted Theodore Roosevelt, Albert Einstein and Zane Grey. This National Historic Landmark has been renovated many times over the years, and today it has wheelchair-accessible rooms with tub/shower combinations.

The main entrance (which faces Hopi House) has steps, but a ramped accessible entrance is located on the canyon side. Just head towards the flagpole, and turn left when you get to the end of the building.

There's good pathway access to the front desk, and level access to the accessible rooms, which are located down a hallway off the main lobby. The El Tovar Hotel has two wheelchair-accessible rooms.

Bedroom in room 6439 at the El Tovar Hotel

Bathroom in room 6439 at the El Tovar Hotel

Bedroom in room 6441 at the El Tovar Hotel

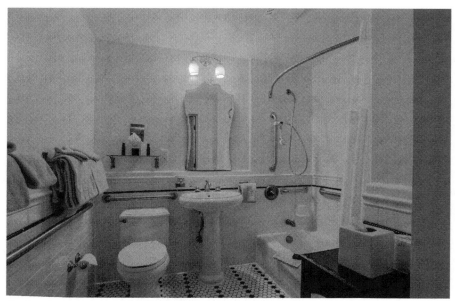

Bathroom in room 6441 at the El Tovar Hotel

Room 6439 has wide doorways, a lowered peephole, low-pile carpet and good pathway access. It's furnished with a 27-inch high king-sized bed with wheelchair access on both sides, two night stands and a refrigerator. There's an accessible pathway to the bathroom, which is equipped with a tub/shower combination, with grab bars, a hand-held showerhead and a portable shower chair. The bathroom also includes a toilet with grab bars on the back and left walls (as seated), and a pedestal sink.

Room 6441 includes the same basic access features as room 6439, but it's a deluxe room and it's a little larger. It's furnished with two 28-inch high queen-sized beds with wheelchair access between them. The bathroom configuration is the same as in room 6439, except that the toilet grab bars are located on the back and right walls (as seated).

There's good pathway access to the public areas of the property as well, including the lobby, dining room and lounge. Accessible restrooms are located in the lobby, and a key is available at the front desk. And for a nice canyon view, there's level access out to the back porch from the hallway off the main lobby.

The El Tovar Hotel is open year-round.

Kachina Lodge

5 North Village Loop Drive
Grand Canyon, AZ 86023
(888) 297-2757
www.grandcanyonlodges.com

Kachina Lodge is located next door to the El Tovar Hotel on the canyon rim. This contemporary property was built in the 1960s, and the brick interior walls reflect the style of the era.

There's no front desk for this property, so guests check-in at the El Tovar Hotel. Kachina Lodge features two wheelchair-accessible rooms, both of which have tub/shower combinations.

Room 6318 features a wide doorway, a lowered peephole, low-pile carpet and good pathway access. It's furnished with a 26-inch high king-sized bed, an easy chair, a desk and a chair, and a chest of drawers. The bathroom has a tub/shower combination with a hand-held showerhead, grab bars and a portable shower chair. The toilet grab bars are located on the back and right walls (as seated). Other access features include a roll-under sink and a lowered mirror.

Room 6320 features the same basic access features as room 6318. It's furnished with a 26-inch high queen-sized bed with wheelchair access on

Bedroom in room 6318 at Kachina Lodge

Bathroom in room 6318 at Kachina Lodge

the right side (as you face it). It has the same bathroom configuration as room 6318, except that the toilet grab bars are located on the back and left walls (as seated).

Bedroom in room 6320 at Kachina Lodge

Bathroom in room 6320 at Kachina Lodge

Both accessible rooms also include electric drapery controls and a refrigerator.

Kachina Lodge is also the only property in the park with an elevator, so it's a good choice for slow walkers who want a standard room on an upper floor (all the accessible rooms are located on the first floor). Additionally, slow walkers who prefer a standard first-floor room should specify that they also require a room along an accessible route, as there are some steps along the first floor corridors.

Kachina Lodge is open year-round.

Thunderbird Lodge

7 North Village Loop Drive
Grand Canyon, AZ 86023
(888) 297-2757
www.grandcanyonlodges.com

Located next door to Kachina Lodge, Thunderbird Lodge is identical in style and ambiance. This property has three wheelchair-accessible rooms, which are equipped with a roll-in shower or a tub/shower combination. It's also the only property in the park that has wheelchair-accessible rooms with canyon views.

Like Kachina Lodge, there's no front desk at Thunderbird Lodge, so guests check-in at the Bright Angel Lodge, which is located next door. Accessible parking is located near the main entrance to Bright Angel Lodge, with ramp access up to the automatic front doors, and a barrier-free pathway over to the front desk. There is also level access to Bright Angel Lodge from the canyon side.

There's level access to room 6213 at Thunderbird Lodge, which features wide doorways, a lowered peephole, low-pile carpet and good pathway access. It's furnished with two 26-inch high queen-sized beds with an access aisle between them, a chest of drawers, and a desk with a chair.

There's a sliding door to the bathroom, which is equipped with a roll-in shower with a hand-held showerhead, grab bars and a portable shower chair. The toilet grab bars are located on the back and right walls (as seated), and the bathroom also has a roll-under sink.

Room 6211 has the same access features and bed configuration as room 6213, except that it also has a second door which opens out to the canyon.

Room 6209 also has the same access features and bed configuration as room 6213, except that the bathroom is equipped with a tub/shower combination.

All three accessible rooms also include electric drapery controls and a refrigerator.

Bedroom in room 6213 at Thunderbird Lodge

Bathroom in room 6213 at Thunderbird Lodge

And like Kachina Lodge, there are some steps along the first-floor corridors, so slow walkers who prefer a standard first-floor room should specify that they also require a room along an accessible route.

Thunderbird Lodge is open year-round.

Maswik Lodge

202 South Village Loop Drive
Grand Canyon, AZ 86023
(888) 297-2757
www.grandcanyonlodges.com

Maswik Lodge is a motel-style property, with parking located right outside the rooms. The property is spread out between buildings dotted throughout a pine forest. Formerly it was divided into a north and south section, but the older south section has been demolished and plans are underway to construct a new lodge complex. The new addition, which will include accessible rooms, is scheduled to be completed in 2021.

The north section has 10 wheelchair-accessible rooms which are equipped with a roll-in shower or a tub/shower combination. Accessible parking is located near the main lobby, with level access to the entrance, and a barrier-free pathway over to the front desk.

Bedroom in room 6761 at Maswik Lodge

Room 6761 is located near the main lodge in the Cliffrose Building. There's accessible parking in front, with level access to the room. Other access features include wide doorways, a lowered peephole, lever handles and a lowered closet rod. It's furnished with two 23-inch high queen-sized beds,

Bathroom in room 6761 at Maswik Lodge

with wheelchair access between them, a chest of drawers, a table with two chairs, and a refrigerator. It also has a sliding glass door, with level access out to a small patio area.

The bathroom has a roll-in shower with grab bars, a hand-held showerhead and a fold-down shower bench. The toilet grab bars are located on the back and left walls (as seated), and the bathroom also has a roll-under sink and a lowered mirror.

Room 6892, which is located in the Spruce Building has the same general access features and bed configuration as room 6761, except that the bathroom is equipped with a tub/shower combination, with grab bars and a portable shower chair. The toilet grab bar configuration and sink location are the same as in room 6761.

Room 6742 is located in the Aspen Building, close to the main lodge. It has the same access features and bed configuration as room 6761, except that the bathroom is equipped with a tub/shower combination with grab bars, a hand-held showerhead and a portable shower chair. The toilet grab bars are located on the back and right walls (as seated), and a large roll-under sink is located just outside of the bathroom. This room also has a sliding glass door that leads out to a patio: however there is one step down to it.

Bathroom in room 6742 at Maswik Lodge

Additionally, there's barrier-free access to all the public areas of Maswik Lodge, including the gift shop and lobby. The Maswik Food Court, which is adjacent to the lobby, features barrier-free access and serves up plated meals, salads, sandwiches and light snacks throughout the day. There is also level access to the Maswik Pizza Pub, which is open for lunch and dinner.

Accessible restrooms are located across from the front desk.

Maswik Lodge is open year-round

Yavapai Lodge

11 Yavapai Lodge Road
Grand Canyon, AZ
(877) 404-4611
www.visitgrandcanyon.com

Located in a pine forest near Market Plaza, Yavapai Lodge features eight wheelchair-accessible rooms equipped with a roll-in shower or a tub/shower combination. The main lodge building is located across the parking lot from Canyon Village Market & Deli. There's accessible parking near the building, with an accessible pathway to the front door and level access to the lobby. Inside there's plenty of room to navigate a wheelchair over to the front desk. The park shuttle bus also stops directly in front of the main lodge building.

Bedroom in room 7426 at Yavapai Lodge

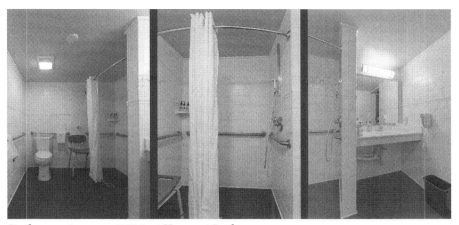

Bathroom in room 7426 at Yavapai Lodge

The accessible rooms are located a short drive away, in the Yavapai East section of the property. Accessible parking is located in front of the buildings, with barrier-free access over to individual rooms.

Room 7426 features a key-operated automatic door, that can also be operated with a closed fist from the inside of the room. Other access features include wide doorways, a lowered peephole, low-pile carpet, a lowered closet rod and good pathway access. The room is furnished with a 30-inch high king-sized bed with wheelchair access on both sides, two

Bedroom in room 7304 at Yavapai Lodge

night stands, an easy chair, a chest of drawers, a desk with a chair and a refrigerator.

A pocket door leads to the bathroom, which is equipped with a roll-in shower with grab bars, a hand-held showerhead and a portable shower chair. The toilet grab bars are located on the back and right walls (as seated), and the bathroom also includes a roll-under sink.

Room 7304 and room 7420 include the same basic access features as room 7426, but they are furnished with two 30-inch high queen-sized beds with wheelchair access between them. The bathroom is equipped with a roll-in shower, with grab bars, a hand-held showerhead and a portable shower bench. The toilet grab bars are located on the back and left walls (as seated), and the bathroom also includes a roll-under sink.

Room 7310 has the same access features and bed configuration as room 7304, but it's a mirror image, so the toilet grab bars are located on the back and right walls (as seated).

Room 7260 has the same basic access features as room 7426. It's furnished with two 30-inch high queen-sized beds, with wheelchair access between them. The bathroom is equipped with a tub/shower combination with grab bars, a hand-held showerhead and a portable shower bench. The toilet grab bars are located on the back and right walls (as seated), and the bathroom also includes a roll-under sink.

Room 7370 is a mirror image of room 7260. It offers the same access features and bed configuration of room 7260, but the toilet grab bars are located on the back and left walls (as seated).

Bathroom in room 7310 at Yavapai Lodge

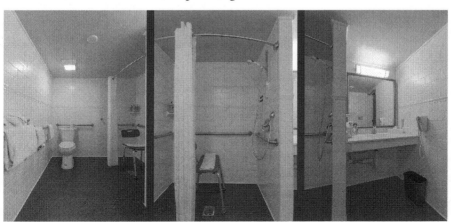

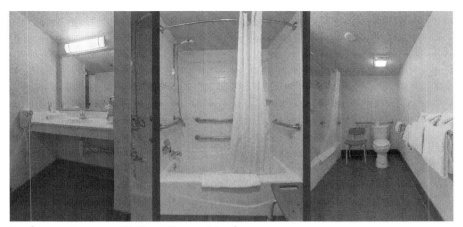

Bathroom in room 7370 at Yavapai Lodge

Room 7254 includes the same basic access features as room 7426. It is furnished with two 30-inch high queen-sized beds with an access aisle between them, and includes a bathroom that is equipped with a tub/shower combination, with grab bars a hand-held showerhead and a portable shower bench. It also has a toilet with grab bars and a roll-under sink.

Room 7376 contains the same basic access features as room 7426. It's furnished with a 30-inch high king-sized bed, with wheelchair access on the left side (as you face it). It also includes a small 18-inch high sleeper sofa. The bathroom is equipped with a tub/shower combination with grab bars, a hand-held showerhead and a portable shower chair. The toilet grab bars are located on the back and left walls (as seated), and the bathroom also has a roll-under sink.

There's also barrier-free access to all the public areas of Yavapai Lodge, including the lobby, gift shop and accessible restrooms in the main lodge building. There's level access to the self-serve Yavapai Lodge Restaurant, and the adjacent Yavapai Tavern. Additionally, there's barrier-free access to the Yavapai Coffee Shop, which is located off the lobby and offers grab-and-go selections for breakfast and lunch.

Yavapai Lodge is open year-round.

Grand Canyon Lodge North Rim

Bridle Path
North Rim, AZ 86052
(877) 386-4383
www.grandcanyonforever.com

The Grand Canyon Lodge North Rim consists of a main lodge building surrounded by rustic cabins dotted throughout a pine forest. There's accessible parking near the main lodge building with level access to the front door, and a barrier-free pathway over to the registration desk. It should be noted that visitors with an accessible parking placard can drive beyond the "no vehicle beyond this point" sign, and park in the accessible parking spots near the front door of the lodge. Porter service for luggage delivery, and guest transportation in golf carts to and from the cabins are also available.

This property features wheelchair-accessible cabins equipped with either a tub/shower combination or a roll-in shower.

Cabin 356 is an accessible Western Cabin, which is located close to the accessible parking area behind the visitor center. There's ramp access up to the roomy front porch which includes two rustic rocking chairs. Access features include wide doorways, lever handles, a lowered closet rod and

Bedroom/Living area in cabin 356 at Grand Canyon Lodge North Rim

Bedroom/living space in cabin 83 at Grand Canyon Lodge North Rim

bed with wheelchair access on the left side (as you face it). Other furnishings include a desk with a chair, and a refrigerator.

The bathroom is equipped with a roll-in shower with grab bars, a hand-held showerhead, and a fold-down shower bench. The toilet grab bars are located on the back and left walls (as seated), and the bathroom also has a roll-under sink.

Cabin 5, which is also an accessible Pioneer Cabin, has the same furnishings and access features as cabin 83, except that the toilet grab bars are located on the back and right walls (as seated). It's also closer to the main lodge, and accessible parking is available in front of the lodge with a level pathway to the room.

Cabin 29 is an accessible Frontier Cabin, which features wide doorways, lever handles and good pathway access. It's located just east of the main lodge building, and there's accessible parking in front of the lodge, with barrier-free access over a paved pathway to the cabin. There's ramp access to the cabin, which is furnished with a 23-inch high double bed with wheelchair access on the left side (as you face it), and a 27-inch high twin bed with wheelchair access on the right side (as you face it), a desk with a chair, and a refrigerator. It's a very large room, with even enough space for a roll away bed.

The bathroom is equipped with a roll-in shower with grab bars, a hand-held

Cabin 5 at Grand Canyon Lodge North Rim

showerhead and a fold-down shower bench. The toilet grab bars are located on the back and left walls (as seated), and the bathroom also has a roll-under sink. Other access features include a lowered robe hook and lowered towel bars.

Cabin 29 at Grand Canyon Lodge North Rim

Bedroom/living space in cabin 29 at Grand Canyon Lodge North Rim

Cabin 84 is also an accessible Frontier Cabin, and it includes the same basic access features as cabin 29. It's furnished with a 26-inch high twin bed, with wheelchair access on the right (as you face it), and a 26-inch high double bed, which can have wheelchair access on either side (it's located in an alcove and

Bathroom in cabin 29 at Grand Canyon Lodge North Rim

Cabin 84 at Grand Canyon Lodge North Rim

can be moved against either wall). The bathroom access features are the same as those in cabin 29, except that the toilet grab bars are located on the back and right walls (as seated).

Bedroom/living space in cabin 84 at Grand Canyon Lodge North Rim

Bathroom in cabin 84 at Grand Canyon Lodge North Rim

There's good pathway access throughout the public spaces on the property, and new accessible cement walkways have been added over the years. The sun porch — which is a prime spot to view the sunset — features level access from the main lodge building. The Grand Canyon Lodge Dining Room features level access, and is open for breakfast, lunch an dinner. There's also a prime rib buffet served in the auditorium, which features lift access. The Roughrider Saloon and Coffee Shop offers ramp access in back; and there's level access to the Deli in the Pines, which is located next to the accessible restrooms. And if you get lost, directional signs point visitors to the wheelchair-accessible routes.

The Grand Canyon Lodge North Rim is open from May 15 to October 15.

Access Overview

Access upgrades have been continually added to the Grand Canyon over the years, and a result there are many accessible choices for wheelchair-users and slow walkers. That said, the South Rim elevation ranges from 7,000 feet to 7,500 feet, while the North Rim tops 8,000 feet, so it's best to take it slow and easy on your first days in the park.

Rim Trail near Yaki Point

There's no shortage of accessible trails on the South Rim, including over 13 miles of a paved multiuse trail, which is ideal for wheelchair-users, slow walkers and handcyclists. Additionally there's a five mile section of the Rim Trail that's wheelchair accessible — from the South Kaibab Trailhead to Hermit Road. And if you'd like a scenic drive, Desert View Drive and Hermit Road (seasonally) offer some great views and a number of accessible overlooks.

On the other hand, wheelchair-users can certainly enjoy the South Rim without a car, as all of the park shuttle buses are equipped with ramps and tie-downs. There are three shuttle bus routes along the South Rim — the Village Route, the Hermits Rest Route and the Kaibab Rim Route — as well as an additional route that runs seasonally from the the Grand Canyon Visitor Center to nearby Tusayan. The Xanterra Travel Collection also operates bus tours along the South Rim, which can be made accessible with 48 hours notice.

And if you'd like to learn a bit about Fred Harvey history, be sure and pop in to the Bright Angel History Room on the South Rim. There's level access to the tiny museum, which is located right off the lobby of the namesake hotel. Exhibits include artifacts from the park's two Harvey Houses — El Tovar Hotel and Bright Angel Lodge — as well as old photos, an 1880 Harvey House dinner gong, and even a vintage Harvey Girl uniform.

Angels Window at Cape Royale

Over on the quieter North Rim, the facilities are not as developed, so you'll definitely need a car to get around. Take some time to wind along the 32-mile Cape Royal Drive, which offers panoramic views up, down and across the canyon, with scenic windshield views at numerous overlooks along the way.

Don't miss the Cape Royal Trail at the end of the line. The paved accessible trail offers some jaw dropping views of the canyon, and a peek-a-boo glimpse of the Colorado River through Angels Window. Alternatively you can sit back and get an equally stunning canyon view from the accessible sun porch at the Grand Canyon Lodge North Rim. Either way, there's no shortage of dramatic scenery in one of America's most popular national parks.

Don't Miss This

For a glimpse of the canyon from yet another vantage point, check out Grand Canyon Scenic Airlines, which offers wheelchair-accessible flightseeing excursions in a fixed-wing Vistaliner aircraft. There are six stairs up to the aircraft door, but a portable ramp is available for anyone who can't manage the climb. Some manual wheelchair-users may need a bit of assistance with the slope of the ramp, but the crew is well versed in setting up the adjustable ramp as the owner's two sons are wheelchair-users.

Boarding ramp at Grand Canyon Scenic Airlines

There's a single seat with extra leg room by the aircraft door, and passengers must have enough trunk support to sit upright in the airplane seat. The 45-minute South Rim Airplane Tour includes views of the Zuni Corridor, Imperial Point, the Confluence of the Colorado and Little Colorado Rivers, Kaibab National Forest and Kaibab Plateau. And you'll get a great view of everything through the large picture windows. Truly it's a bucket list item — one that many folks pass up because they don't think it's accessible — and a must-do on any Grand Canyon visit.

Insider Tip

Yaki Point on the South Rim offers some nice windshield views of the canyon, and it's a popular alternative to Mather Point for a sunrise photo stop. Unfortunately, private vehicles are prohibited along the road to Yaki Point, and the sunrise bus tours and shuttles fill up quickly. The good news is, disabled visitors can get a Scenic Drive Accessibility Permit and drive their own vehicles down to Yaki Point to enjoy the sunrise. It's the easy, quick and independent way to take in the canyon view. And the permit is also good along Hermit Road, when it's closed to private vehicles from March 1 to November 30. Best of all, there's no charge for the permit, which is available at park entrances, visitor centers and park hotels.

Resources

Grand Canyon National Park

(928) 638-7888

www.nps.gov/grca

www.facebook.com/GrandCanyonNationalPark

twitter.com/GrandCanyonNPS

Road Conditions

(928) 638-7496

Xanterra Travel Collection (NPS Concessionaire)

(888) 297-2757

www.grandcanyonlodges.com

www.facebook.com/grandcanyonlodges

El Tovar Hotel

Thunderbird Lodge

Kachina Lodge

Maswik Lodge

Delaware North (NPS Concessionaire)

(877) 404-4611

www.visitgrandcanyon.com

Yavapai Lodge

Forever Resorts (NPS Concessionaire)

(877) 386-4383

www.grandcanyonforever.com

www.facebook.com/GrandCanyonNorthRim

Grand Canyon Lodge North Rim

Grand Canyon Scenic Airlines

3555 Airport Road

Grand Canyon (Tusayan), AZ 86023

(800) 634-6801

www.scenic.com

Barrier-Free Travel; The Grand Canyon for Wheelers and Slow Walkers
www.BarrierFreeGrandCanyon.com

California

Tunnel View in Yosemite National Park

Death Valley National Park

L ocated on a remote stretch of land in Eastern California, Death Valley National Park is about a two hour drive from Las Vegas, and a four-hour drive from Las Angeles. Not only is it the hottest, driest and lowest point in North America, but this three-million acre preserve is the largest national park in the lower 48 states. From windblown sand dunes and eerie salt flats, to snow capped peaks, a lush oasis and even a massive crater, there's something for just about everyone at this off-the-beaten -path national treasure. Although the name sounds a bit foreboding, the park also boasts a number of accessible trails, attractions and scenic drives for wheelchair-users and slow walkers. And thanks to some recent access upgrades by park concessionaires, there's no shortage of accessible lodging is this expansive desert retreat.

There are no entrance stations at Death Valley National Park — visitors pay their entrance fees at automated kiosks or at the visitor center — however there are several roads that lead to the national park.

On the west side of the park Highway 178 connects to Highway 190 and enters the park just east of Panamint Springs. This West Entrance is about 70 miles northeast of Ridgecrest. Alternatively, Highway 190 begins in

Badwater, Death Valley — the lowest point in North America

Olancha and travels 40 miles east to the West Entrance. This entrance is also 50 miles southeast of Lone Pine and can also be accessed by Highway 136 which connects to Highway 190.

On the south side of the park, Highway 127 runs from Interstate 15 to the Shoshone Entrance, which is about 85 miles north of Baker.

Over on the east side of the park, Highway 374 runs from Highway 95 to the Northeast Entrance, about 13 miles southwest of Beatty. Highway 95 also connects to Highway 373 in Lathrop Wells. The road transitions to Highway 127 when it enters California, connects with Highway 190 at Death Valley Junction, and continues on to the East Entrance. This route is about 33 miles long. Alternatively, Highway 267 leads from Scotty's Junction at Highway 95 and travels 26 miles southwest to the Scotty's Castle Entrance.

Although Death Valley is open year-round, Dante's View Road and Upper Wildrose Road can close in the winter due to snow and ice. Badwater Road, portions of Highway 190 and Scotty's Castle Road into Grapevine Canyon are subject to flooding and can close after heavy rains. The official park website is usually updated when new closures occur, and the The Death Valley Road Conditions Facebook Page is also a good source for road information.

There are three accessible lodges in Death Valley National Park; two in Furnace Creek, and one in Stovepipe Wells.

Admission

$30 – seven-day pass
$55 – yearly pass

Spend the Night
Inn at Death Valley

CA 190
Death Valley, CA 92328
(800) 236-7916
www.oasisatdeathvalley.com

Nestled into the mountainside, the historic Inn at Death Valley offers a commanding desert view framed by the towering Panamint Mountains. This property received a major renovation in 2018, when it was completely gutted and redone from top to bottom. The result is a modern AAA Four Diamond Inn that exudes an aura of casual elegance. It combines the best of both worlds — the rugged old west and the modern 21st century. And with more green space, less cement and a new grove of date palms, it's a verdant, relaxing and luxurious place to spend a few nights.

Although steps grace the front entrance of this 1927 property, there's elevator access up to the lobby on the side of the building, just around the corner from the valet stand. There's also accessible parking behind the building, with level access through the tunnel to an elevator.

Bedroom in room 323 at the Inn at Death Valley

Bathroom in room 323 at the Inn at Death Valley

There's barrier-free access throughout the third-floor lobby, and excellent views of the surrounding desert from just about anywhere on this floor. Accessible restrooms are located near the registration desk, and there's good pathway access to the historic lobby library, which is filled with comfortable furniture.

The Inn at Death Valley has accessible rooms, casitas, and a suite. Room 323, which is located on the lobby level, features wide doorways, lever handles, low-pile carpet and good pathway access. It's furnished with a 23-inch high king-sized bed with wheelchair access on both sides. Other furnishings include a desk with a chair, two night stands, a refrigerator, and an easy chair.

The bathroom features a full five-foot turning radius and is equipped with a roll-in shower with grab bars, a hand-held showerhead and a fold-down shower bench. Other access features include a toilet with grab bars on the back and left walls (as seated), and a roll-under sink. Top it off with a lowered robe hook, and you have a very accessible room.

The new casitas are located a short drive away from the main lobby; however casita guests are issued their own golf carts at check-in. If a guest is unable to drive a golf cart, valet service to and from the casita is available.

Casita 501 is an accessible casita. Access features include wide doorways, lever handles and excellent pathway access. The casita includes a living area that's furnished with a 13-inch high sleeper sofa, a desk with a chair, an easy chair and a chest of drawers. Around the corner there's a wet bar with a refrigerator and a microwave. There's also level access out to the spacious patio which borders an expansive lawn area. The patio includes a table with chairs, but there's still plenty of room for a wheelchair.

Casita 501 at the Inn at Death Valley

The bedroom is furnished with two 22-inch high queen-sized beds with an access aisle between them, a chest of drawers and a night stand. The spacious bathroom is equipped with a roll-in shower with grab bars, a hand-held showerhead and a fold-down shower bench located close to the

Bedroom in Casita 501 at the Inn at Death Valley

Living room in Casita 501 at the Inn at Death Valley

shower controls. The toilet grab bars are located on the back and left walls (as seated) and the bathroom also includes a roll-under sink.

This casita adjoins another accessible casita that has the same basic access features, but it's furnished with a king-sized bed. The accessible casitas are also located near the lift-equipped swimming pool; however there's also an accessible parking place in front of the pool if you'd prefer to drive. These new casitas at the Inn at Death Valley are the most accessible and luxurious accommodations in the park.

Bathroom in Casita 501 at the Inn at Death Valley

There's good wheelchair access to the public areas of the inn, including the restaurant, bar and the new library. Even if you don't stay at the property, stop in for a bite to eat or a drink, and enjoy the expansive view of the lush grounds, towering palms and the desert in the distance.

The Inn at Death Valley is open year-round.

Ranch at Death Valley

CA 190
Death Valley, CA 92328
(800) 236-7916
www.oasisatdeathvalley.com

Originally a working ranch, the Ranch at Death Valley welcomed its first guests in 1933. A family-friendly favorite for years, the property received a major facelift in 2018, with a $100 million renovation project. Not only did this massive undertaking modernize the facilities, but it also added new amenities to the property. Today two new Spanish Colonial Revival buildings grace the entrance, and house the registration area, new restaurants and a well-stocked store. Add in some lush new landscaping, and you have a totally revitalized property.

Accessible parking is available in front of the new registration building,

Registration desk at the Ranch at Death Valley

which is located right off Highway 190. There's barrier-free access to the front door, and good pathway access over to the registration desk. The new town square park — a relaxing green space with accessible pathways and benches — borders the registration building on the hotel side of the building.

The Ranch at Death Valley has four accessible rooms with roll-in showers and four accessible rooms with tub/shower combinations. Room 402, which is a deluxe accessible room, is located a short walk from the office, near the swimming pool and sports courts. Accessible parking is located near the room, with barrier-free access to the front door.

Access features include wide doorways, lever handles, low-pile carpet and good pathway access. The room is furnished with a 25-inch high full bed and a 25-inch high twin bed, with an access aisle between them. Other furnishings include a desk with a chair, a chest of drawers, an easy chair and a refrigerator. There's also a sliding glass door that leads out to a shared patio, and offers a refreshing view of the verdant lawn, with the mountains in the distance. There's plenty of room for a wheelchair on the patio, and there's level access from inside.

The bathroom boasts a full five-foot turning radius and is equipped with a roll-in shower with grab bars, a hand-held showerhead and a built-in corner shower seat. The toilet grab bars are located on the back and right

Bedroom in room 402 at the Ranch at Death Valley (view 1)

Bedroom in room 402 at the Ranch at Death Valley (view 2)

walls (as seated), and the bathroom also includes a roll-under sink.

The property is spread out, but accessible pathways lead to and from the rooms and all of the facilities. There's good access to the public areas of

Bathroom in room 402 at the Ranch at Death Valley

the hotel, including the restaurants, General Store, Trading Post and golf course. There's ramp access to the pool area, and barrier-free access to the lift-equipped pool, showers and changing rooms. There are also two accessible picnic tables located in the level picnic area adjacent to the bus parking area. All in all, the Ranch at Death Valley is a very comfortable and accessible property.

The Ranch at Death Valley is open year-round.

Stovepipe Wells Village Hotel

51880 CA 190
Death Valley, CA 92328
(760) 786-7090
deathvalleyhotels.com

This historic hotel, which sports a decidedly western theme, has been serving Death Valley visitors since 1926. Access improvements are continually added to this comfortable property; including a recently installed lowered check-in counter in the office. The staff is friendly, the rooms are comfortable, and you just can't beat the desert views. This 83-room hotel has two accessible rooms with roll-in showers, and two semi-accessible rooms with low-step showers.

Bedroom in room 50 at Stovepipe Wells Village Hotel

Accessible parking is located in front of the gift shop with level access over to the registration desk, which is located behind the business center. The two accessible rooms are located a short walk away, near the pool and close to the restaurant and saloon. Accessible parking is also available in front of accessible rooms 49 and 50, with barrier-free access over to each room.

Room 50 features wide doorways, lever handles, low-pile carpet, and barrier-free pathways throughout the unit. It's furnished with two 26-inch high open-frame full beds, with wheelchair access on all sides. Other furnishings include an easy chair, a chest of drawers, and a small refrigerator.

The spacious bathroom includes a full five-foot turning radius, and is equipped with a large roll-in shower with a grab bars, a handheld showerhead and a fold-down shower seat. Other access features include a toilet with grab bars on the back and left walls (as seated), and a roll-under sink.

Room 49 has the same basic access features, except that the toilet grab bars are located on the back and right walls (as seated). This room has a slightly different configuration, as the furniture is placed differently; however it still offers excellent pathway access.

Bathroom in room 50 at Stovepipe Wells Village Hotel

Bathroom in room 49 at Stovepipe Wells Village Hotel

Room 74, which is located on the other side of the complex, may work for some slow walkers. Parking is available directly in front of the room, with barrier-free access to the front door. Access features include wide doorways, lever handles, low-pile carpet, and good pathway access throughout the unit.

Bedroom in room 74 at Stovepipe Wells Village Hotel

Bathroom in room 74 at Stovepipe Wells Village Hotel

Furnishings include a 26-inch high open-frame king-sized bed with wheelchair access on both sides, an easy chair, a chest of drawers and a refrigerator. There's also a second door that opens up to a shared back patio, and includes plenty of room for a wheelchair or scooter. Bathroom access features include a low-step (two-inch) shower and toilet grab bars on the back and left walls (as seated).

There's barrier-free access to all the public areas of the hotel, including the restaurants and the gift shop. Wi-Fi is available in the accessible business center, and although the signal is weak, it's good enough for e-mail. There's also barrier-free access to the swimming pool, which includes a portable wheelchair-lift. This rustic property captures the spirit of Death Valley and offers good wheelchair access.

Stovepipe Wells Village Hotel is open year-round.

Access Overview

Although tall peaks surround Death Valley, the bulk of the national park has an elevation near sea level. That said, the elevation up at Dante's View is 5,475 feet, so if you are unsure of the effects of higher altitudes on your body, take it a slow and drink plenty of water up there.

Furnace creek has a number of accessible trails and attractions, including the outdoor Borax Museum at the Ranch at Death Valley. There's barrier-free access on the side of the museum, with good pathway access around the rail cars, mining equipment and tools that help tell the story of Borax mining in the valley.

Harmony Borax Works, which is located near the visitor center, contains the ruins of a borax refinery. It's a .20-mile walk to the lower exhibits, which include a 20 mule team wagon which was used to haul borax out of Death Valley, and the remains of the refinery. From there, the trail continues uphill and loops around to the other side of the refinery, and offers a closer look at the equipment. Some manual wheelchair-users may require assistance because of the grade of the upper trail; however even if you can't manage the whole trail, the trek out to the lower exhibit is worth the walk. All in all it's a half-mile loop.

And although there's accessible parking near Harmony Borax Works, if

Harmony Borax Works in Death Valley

you'd like to walk, there's a 1.5-mile accessible bicycle path that begins at the visitor center and offers some nice mountain views on the way to the borax works.

One of the most accessible trails in the park, Salt Creek Boardwalk, is located west of Harmony Borax Works, off of Highway 190. The half-mile round trip trail winds around Salt Creek, which is home to the indigenous pupfish. Although the creek dries up in the summer, you'll usually find water there from November through May.

There's no shortage of breathtaking views in the park, including Zabriskie Point, which is off Highway 190 just east of the Inn at Furnace Creek. The trail up to the viewpoint is just 100-yards long, but it may be too steep for manual wheelchair-users. That said if you can make it to the top you'll be rewarded with a panoramic view of the badlands with the salt flats in the distance.

One of the best views in the park is located just up the road at Dante's View. An accessible sidewalk leads around the viewpoint where you'll see Badwater Basin, the Panamint Range and Telescope Peak to the west, and the Greenwater Range on the east.

Badwater, the lowest point in North America, is also worth a visit. From the parking area there's ramp access out to a short boardwalk out to the salt

Salt Creek Boardwalk in Death Valley

Artists Drive in Death Valley

flats. There's also level access over to the Badwater sign — a popular photo spot — which touts the elevation of 282 feet below sea level. There's a well trod level path out across the salt flats, as a result of years of foot traffic. The entire trail is a little over a mile long, but as you get farther out it gets bumpier, due to less traffic. The first quarter-mile is pretty tramped down and doable for most wheelchair-users and slow walkers. Don't forget to look up to get a gander at Dante's View, which is precariously perched some 5,000 feet above the salt flats.

One of the most scenic drives in the park — Artists Drive — is located near Badwater. This one-way nine-mile drive winds up through the colorful mountains and offers an up-close-and-personal view of this scenic Death Valley landscape. One of the highlights of the drive is the Artists Palette overlook, which is located off the main road. There's accessible parking in the small lot, and a barrier-free path over to the interpretive plaque. The volcanic minerals in the hills, which have been chemically altered by the extreme heat, cause the vibrant hillside colors. It is indeed a colorful palette.

Up near Stovepipe Wells, be sure and stop at the Mesquite Flat Sand Dunes for a good look at the desert landscape. You can get a good view of the dunes from the accessible parking spot; however there is a 250-foot hard-packed dirt trail that leads out to the brink of the dunes and offers a different perspective on the area.

And Don't miss Devil's Cornfield, which is just down the road from the sand dunes. There's no accessible parking, but paved level pullouts are located on both sides of the road, near an interpretive plaque. Although the plants resemble bundled corn left to dry, they are actually arrowweed plants that have adapted to their harsh desert environment. The high winds in the area have scoured the sand away from the roots of the plants and left a pedestal of dirt and exposed roots at their bases, thus giving them their strange haystack look.

Don't Miss This

Most folks zip right on by 20 Mule Team Canyon, on their way to visit the more popular Dante's View on Highway 190. So make sure and take this 2.5-mile drive that winds up and down through the colorful eroded badlands, and offers an off-the-beaten-track experience without having to trek through the desert for days. This one-way dirt road is graded, and suitable for even low clearance vehicles. That said, it closes during heavy rains as it's subject to flooding. Interestingly enough this narrow road was never traversed by the infamous 20 mule teams, as it wasn't wide enough to accommodate them. There aren't really any places to stop and park along the drive, but the windshield views are excellent. And if there aren't any cars

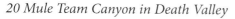

20 Mule Team Canyon in Death Valley

behind you, you can always roll down the window and snap a few photos. Although the drive is pretty short the road winds up and down through the badlands, so it takes about 30 minutes to complete. It's a great stop after Zabriskie Point, on the way to Dante's View.

Insider Tip

Death Valley is the perfect place to enjoy a picnic lunch al fresco while you explore all that the national park has to offer. That said, there is an extreme shortage of sheltered picnic tables in the park, and that can present some problems with the intense midday sun. And although most of the picnic areas are marked on the park map, two new information stations that have covered picnic tables are not. They both include an accessible parking space and curb-cut access up to an accessible vault toilet. And although they are located along main roads, they offer excellent desert views, and make a good stop for a pleasant lunch. One information station is located near the intersection of Mud Canyon and the Beatty Cutoff (Hell's Gate); while the other is located on Scotty's Castle Road, just north of Highway 374. So add them to your accessible picnic site list, and enjoy your noon meal in shaded comfort.

View at Zabriskie Point in Death Valley

Resources

Death Valley National Park
(760) 786-3200
www.nps.gov/deva/index.htm
www.facebook.com/DeathValleyNPS/
twitter.com/DeathValleyNPS

Death Valley Road Conditions
www.facebook.com/DeathValleyRoadConditions

Xanterra Travel Collection (NPS Concessionaire)
(800) 236-7916
www.oasisatdeathvalley.com
www.facebook.com/oasisatdeathvalley/
twitter.com/FurnaceCreekRes
The Inn at Death Valley
The Ranch at Death Valley

Death Valley Lodging Company (NPS Concessionaire)
(760) 786-7090
deathvalleyhotels.com
Stovepipe Wells Resort

Kings Canyon National Park

This Central California park, which is located 50 miles northeast of Visalia, is often overlooked in the rush to visit nearby Yosemite. As a result, the crowd factor is much lower at Kings Canyon National Park, and visitors can enjoy the surrounding natural beauty in relative solitude.

The park itself consists of two distinct regions — Grant Grove and Cedar Grove — which are connected by the Kings Canyon Scenic Byway that runs through the adjacent Sequoia National Forest. Grant Grove is known for its giant sequoias, while Cedar Grove boasts some magnificent granite canyons. And even though the park is well off-the-beaten-path, it still boasts a number of accessible trails and overlooks where visitors can get up-close-and-personal with the towering trees and enjoy the sweeping canyon views.

Technically the park only has one official entrance — the Big Stump Entrance — which is located on Highway 180, about an hour east of Fresno. From the park entrance it's a 15-minute drive to Grant Grove, and another hour drive to Cedar Grove. Alternatively visitors can access the park via the Generals Highway, which passes through the Sequoia National Forest from Sequoia National Park.

Kings Canyon National Park is open year-round, but Highway 180 is closed in the winter, six miles east of Grant Grove Village. This road generally reopens in April, however late snowfalls may delay the opening; so it's always a good idea to check the road conditions in both the national park and the national forest. And always carry chains or cables, as they may be required at any time from early fall to late spring due to snow and ice on the roads. Keep in mind that weather conditions can and do change quickly in this neck of the woods.

There are three lodges in Kings Canyon National Park; two in Grant Grove and one in Cedar Grove.

Admission
(also includes admission to Sequoia National Park)

$35 – seven-day pass
$70 – yearly pass

Spend the Night

John Muir Lodge

86728 Highway 180
Kings Canyon National Park, CA 93633
(866) 807-3598
www.visitsequoia.com

This classic stone and timber lodge is located a short drive uphill from the Kings Canyon Visitor Center, just past the road that leads to Panoramic Point. The 36-room mountain property, which was built in 1998, boasts the best of both worlds; as not only does it offer all the comforts of home, but it's also located in the middle of a beautiful sequoia and pine forest. And although John Muir Lodge is open year-round, the snowy winters that are common in this area make access difficult for wheelchair-users and slow walkers during that time.

Accessible parking is available in front of the lodge, with level access over to the accessible entrance on the left side of the building. From there, the porch winds around to the front entrance, which has a level threshold and wide double doors. A large stone fireplace graces the front lobby, and there's plenty of room to navigate a wheelchair around the furnishings.

Accessible room 114 is located just around the corner, through a hallway lined

John Muir Lodge in Kings Canyon National Park

Bedroom in room 114 at John Muir Lodge in Kings Canyon National Park

with vintage photos of the giant forest. Access features in the room include wide doorways, a lowered peephole and good pathway access. It's furnished with a 25-inch high open-frame bed with wheelchair access on both sides, a table with two chairs, an easy chair, a chest of drawers and a refrigerator.

Bathroom in room 114 at John Muir Lodge in Kings Canyon National Park

There's barrier-free access to the bathroom, which is outfitted with a tub/shower combination with grab bars, a hand-held showerhead and a fold-down wooden slatted bench at the far end of the tub. The toilet has grab bars on the back and right walls (as seated), and a roll-under sink is located just outside the bathroom.

Room 110 has the same access features as room 114. Both of the accessible rooms are located on the first floor.

There's also barrier-free access to a nice deck that overlooks the forest at the end of the first-floor hallway. Accessible family restrooms — complete with Sharps containers — are located near the front lobby, and the comfortable lodge also features level access to a wide front porch lined with rocking chairs, benches and gliders.

A Continental breakfast buffet, which is served in front of the fireplace, is included with the room rate. And as an added bonus, Wi-Fi access is available to lodge guests in the public areas of the lodge — and that's a coveted amenity that's not routinely found in the area.

Additional dining facilities and shops are located near the visitor center, which features accessible parking and barrier-free access. John Muir Lodge is a comfortable and accessible pick for any Kings Canyon visit.

John Muir Lodge is open year-round.

Grant Grove Cabins

86728 Highway 180
Kings Canyon National Park, CA 93633
(866) 807-3598
www.visitsequoia.com

Located in the meadow below John Muir Lodge, the Grant Grove Cabins offer a more rustic lodging experience in Grant Grove Village. Check-in for these cabins is available in the accessible John Muir Lodge lobby. And although these cabins — with and without bathrooms — are just a short walk away, it's best to drive there, as it's a steep downhill trek.

Meadow Camp cabin 511 features parking on a level pad near the front door, and ramp access up to the one-room cabin. Accessible parking is also available directly across from the cabin, with an accessible pathway through the paved parking lot to the cabin.

This rustic cabin is furnished with 3 full beds. Around back there's a cement patio with a slight one-inch lip. The covered patio is furnished with a picnic table and a small wood stove, and it's a great place to relax and listen to the sounds of the forest in the evening.

The bathhouse is a short walk away, over a paved accessible sidewalk. Accessible family restrooms — again equipped with Sharps containers — are located on one side of the building, while pay showers are located on the opposite end. There's level access to the accessible shower room, which features a roll-in shower with grab bars, a hand-held showerhead and a padded fold-down shower bench. The shower is nicely done, and it allows for independent access, as the hand-held showerhead is within easy reach of the shower seat. There's also room for even the largest wheelchair in the spacious unit.

This historic national park cabin is the perfect choice for wheelchair-users and slow walkers who want some basic creature comforts, yet still enjoy being surrounded by Mother Nature.

Although this property is open year-round, the accessible cabin is not insulated, and is closed during the winter months.

Cabin 511 at Grant Grove Cabins in Kings Canyon National Park

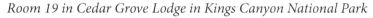

Cedar Grove Lodge

86724 Highway 180
Kings Canyon National Park, CA 93633
(866) 807-3598
www.visitsequoia.com

This humble 21-room property is located an hour from the Grant Grove giant sequoias, in a magnificent glaciated canyon on the banks of the scenic Kings River. Because of heavy snows in this area, the road to Cedar Grove is closed in the winter months; but from summer to fall, this comfortable lodge serves as a convenient home base for the exploration of the more remote canyon section of the park.

Accessible parking is available near the lodge building, with a barrier-free path over to cement and wooden ramps which lead up to the main entrance on the second floor. There are wide doors that lead into the market and the Cedar Grove Café; and the registration desk is located to the left of the doors, across from the market. There's also a lowered pay phone located in front of the lodge.

Although the lodge does not have any accessible rooms, room 19 may work for some slow walkers. This corner room is located on the first floor, which can be accessed from a short level brick pathway that begins near

Room 19 in Cedar Grove Lodge in Kings Canyon National Park

the base of the access ramp to the second floor. There's a wide doorway at the end of the pathway, which leads to into a hallway that allows access to three oversized patio rooms. Room 19 is located at the end of the hallway.

The room features wide doorways and level access from the hallway, and is furnished with a 26-inch high open-frame queen-sized bed, a table with two chairs, and a bedside table. It also has a wet bar with a microwave and a small refrigerator.

The bathroom isn't large enough to accommodate a wheelchair, but there's room in front of it to park a walker in the wide entry hall. The bathroom is equipped with a low-step (six inch) shower, and a standard toilet and sink.

A second door opens out to a semi-private patio that features a nice view

Bathroom in room 19 in Kings Canyon National Park at Cedar Grove Lodge

Room 19 patio in Cedar Grove Lodge in Kings Canyon National Park

of the Kings River. It's furnished with lounge chairs and a picnic table; and although there's a two-inch step up into the room from the patio, it can also be accessed from the brick pathway to the hallway door.

This room is a good choice for slow walkers who cannot navigate stairs, but who don't need any other adaptive features. The patio is also a very relaxing place, as the sound of the nearby river almost lulls you to sleep.

Cedar Grove Lodge is open from May to October.

Access Overview

Although a good percentage of Kings Canyon National Park is composed of rugged backcountry, access features have been added to both the national park and the national forest area. The park itself includes a number of peaks in excess of 10,000 feet in the rugged backcountry, however the glacier-carved valley is a more manageable 4,600 feet. Add in the sequoia forests at 6,600 feet and you definitely have a range of altitudes.

One of the main attractions in the park – the 1,700 year old General Grant Tree – can be seen from an accessible half-mile loop trail that leads through the grove. Not only can visitors get a close look at the 268-foot tall giant, but they can also take in the Gamlin Cabin, the Centennial Stump and

Zumwalt Meadow trail in Cedar Grove

The General Grant Tree in Kings Canyon National Park

the Fallen Monarch from the trail. Even if you can't manage the trail, don't miss scenic Grant Grove Drive which leads from Highway 180 to the grove. There are several accessible pullouts along the way, and there's no shortage of impressive windshield views on the route.

Over in Cedar Grove, the Zumwalt Meadow trail is a nice accessible choice. The first mile of this trail features hard-packed dirt paths and an accessible boardwalk through the meadow, and makes a good out-and-back two-mile hike. And if you can't manage the whole hike, then do the .2-mile jaunt out to the suspension bridge, as it features a particularly pleasant view of the Kings River. While you're in the area, be sure and stop at Roaring River Falls, which is located midway between Knapp's Cabin and Zumwalt Meadow. The .2-mile trail, which ends at the base of the falls, is a good choice for power wheelchair-users, but some manual wheelchair-users made need assistance because of the grade. And you just can't beat the view.

Don't Miss This

Although many people enjoy the drive along the Kings Canyon Scenic Byway, most folks roll right past a few accessible stops on their way to Cedar Grove. Indian Basin Trail, which is located just off the byway near the Princess Campground, tops the list.

Indian Basin Trail

The trail itself has excellent access, as it's wide and paved and meanders through a forest area dotted with giant sequoia stumps. This area was logged in the early 1900s by the Sanger Lumber Company, and all the mature trees were removed at that time. Today young sequoias have replaced many of the logged giants, and the area is filled with wildlife, including birds, squirrels and other small animals. Interpretive panels are located along the 2/3-mile loop, which winds through several meadows and near a secluded aspen grove.

Grizzly Falls Picnic Area also makes a nice stop, even if you don't have a picnic lunch. There's a short paved loop that leads around several accessible picnic tables on cement pads, and there's an excellent view of the falls about 100 feet up the path. And the great news is, you can get a good falls view from any of the picnic tables or even from the parking lot, so be sure and stop.

Insider Tip

The road to Panoramic Point is easy to miss, but the view from the end is well worth the drive. The two-mile road to Panoramic Point is located on the far side of the Grant Grove Visitor Center – just follow the signs to John Muir Lodge, and make a sharp right just before you reach the lodge. The

The trail to Panoramic Point

narrow and winding road is paved, but it lacks a center stripe, and in many spots it's only a one-lane road.

At the end of the line, a quarter-mile trail leads out to Panoramic Point. Although the average trail grade along this wide paved trail is 6.5%, the top grade is 8.5%, so manual wheelchair-users will probably require some assistance. That said, it's perfectly doable for power wheelchair- and scooter-users. Up on top you'll be treated to a magnificent view of Kings Canyon National Park, with Hume Lake, Spanish Mountain and Mt. Goddard clearly visible in the distance. It's definitely worth the short walk, and there are usually not many people up there.

Resources

Kings Canyon National Park
(559) 565-3341
www.nps.gov/seki
www.facebook.com/SequoiaKingsNPS
twitter.com/@sequoiakingsnps

Kings Canyon National Park Road Conditions
(559) 565-3341, then press 1

Sierra National Forest Road Conditions
CalTrans
(800) 427-7623

Delaware North (NPS Concessionaire)
(866) 807-3598
www.visitsequoia.com
John Muir Lodge
Grant Grove Cabins
Cedar Grove Lodge

Barrier-Free Travel; Yosemite, Sequoia and Kings Canyon National Parks for Wheelers and Slow Walkers
www.barrierfreeyosemite.com

Sequoia National Park

Connected to Kings Canyon National Park by the Generals Highway, Sequoia National Park is home to a large grove of giant sequoia trees, including the 275-foot tall General Sherman Tree, the largest tree on Earth. And although technically the park is grouped together with Kings Canyon National Park with a hyphenated name, it's treated as a separate entity for the purposes of this book.

The folks at Sequoia National Park have long been proactive about improving their access. In fact Chief Park Naturalist, William Tweed once told me, "Access isn't just about people with disabilities. It's also about families with small children, and moms with strollers, and people who just walk a little slower. Good accessibility benefits everybody in the long run." And I'm happy to report that this stellar attitude still prevails today.

There are two official entrance stations to Sequoia National Park. The Ash Mountain Entrance, which is located off Highway 198, 35 miles northeast of Visalia, is the main park entrance. From there visitors can access the Giant Forest, then exit the park and continue on along the Generals Highway through Sequoia National Forest to Kings Canyon National Park. There's also a Lookout Point Entrance located southeast of the Ash Mountain Entrance, on the road to Mineral King. Although you'll definitely need a car to explore this remote area of the park, it's well worth the 1.5-hour drive.

Sequoia National Park is open year-round. That said, the Generals Highway — the main road through the park — may close occasionally after winter snow storms, in order to plow the road. The road to Mineral King is not plowed in the winter, and it is usually open from late May to late October. Chains or cables may be required at any time from early fall to late spring due to snow and ice on all park roads.

There is one lodge in Sequoia National Park.

Admission

(also includes admission to Kings Canyon National Park)

$35 – seven-day pass
$70 – yearly pass

Spend the Night
Wuksachi Lodge

64740 Wuksachi Way
Sequoia National Park, CA 93262
(866) 807-3598
www.visitsequoia.com

Wuksachi Lodge, which is located four miles north of the Giant Forest, is open year-round. That said, you'll find the best wheelchair access at this modern mountain lodge from spring through fall, as snow and ice make getting around some of the property pathways very difficult — if not dangerous — in the winter. The 102-room stone-and-cedar lodge blends nicely into the surrounding pine forest, with the main lodge building surrounded by three low-profile buildings that contain the guestrooms. And although Wuksachi Lodge makes the perfect home base for a Sequoia visit, it's also a nice place to grab a bite to eat after an energetic morning hike through the Giant Forest.

Accessible parking is available near the main lodge building, with a paved pathway up to the front door. Inside, there's barrier-free access throughout the inviting lobby to the front desk. The lodge rooms are located 100 to 200

Wuksachi Lodge in Sequoia National Park

yards from the main building, and although there are pathways to and from the outbuildings, some paths are paved, while others are composed of sand and dirt. That said, an accessible on-demand transfer service is available for guests who cannot manage the trails to and from the main lodge. Luggage valet service is also available from the main lodge.

Accessible parking for lodge guests is located in the parking lot on the right, in front of the buildings that house the guestrooms. Best bet is to park in the accessible spaces near the right end for access to the Sequoia and Silliman Buildings. If, on the other hand, your room is in the Stewart building, the accessible parking spaces near the center of the lot are the closest option. Although stairs lead up to the buildings from the parking lot, there's also a paved pathway that winds around the stairs for wheelchair access. And if you can't do distances, use the accessible transfer service, which will take you directly to your building door.

Wuksachi Lodge has eight accessible rooms, all of which have roll-in showers. Rooms 119, 125 and 126 are located in the Stewart Building; rooms 217, 221 and 222 are located in the Silliman Building; and rooms 302 and 305 are located in the Sequoia Building.

Room 305 is a deluxe accessible room. Access features include wide doorways, a lowered peephole, lever handles and good pathway access throughout the unit. It's furnished with a 26-inch high king-sized bed with

Bedroom in room 305 at Wuksachi Lodge

Bathroom in room 305 at Wuksachi Lodge

wheelchair access on both sides, and a 13-inch high sleeper sofa. Other furnishings include a desk with a chair, a chest of drawers, two night tables, a refrigerator and a coffee maker.

The bathroom features a wide pocket door and a full five-foot turning radius. It's equipped with a roll-in shower with grab bars, a hand-held showerhead and a padded fold-down shower bench. The shower is very nicely designed, and the shower controls are easily reachable from the shower seat. Other bathroom access features include a roll-under sink and toilet grab bars on the back and left walls (as seated). Room 125 and room 221 are also accessible deluxe king rooms.

Room 222 is an accessible superior room, and it contains the same general access features as room 305. It's furnished with a 26-inch high king-sized bed with wheelchair access on both sides, as well as a table and two chairs, and two night tables. The 13-inch high sleeper sofa is located in a separate alcove that can be closed off with sliding doors. A refrigerator, coffee maker and a chest of drawers are also located in the alcove. The bathroom has the same access features as room 305, except that the toilet grab bars are located on the back and right walls (as seated). Because the alcove affords more privacy, this room is a good choice for anyone traveling with an attendant. Room 126 is also an accessible superior king room.

Room 119, 217 and 302 are accessible queen rooms.

There's good wheelchair access to the public areas of the main lodge as well, including barrier-free access to a small gift shop just off the lobby, which carries essential sundries, souvenirs, works by local artists and even wine. There's also level access to the Peaks Restaurant and the lobby bar which are

Bedroom in room 222 at Wuksachi Lodge

just around the corner from the front desk. Accessible restrooms are located across from the lobby bar, and there's elevator access to the conference rooms on the lower level.

Alcove in room 222 at Wuksachi Lodge

There's also a nice paved accessible path that leads from the lower level out to the amphitheater and over to a scenic bridge. Ranger programs, nightly s'mores and other interpretive programs are presented in the amphitheater, which features level access and plenty of room for wheelchairs in front. And even if you don't attend any of the programs, the path still makes for a scenic stroll, as the view from the bridge is second-to-none.

Wuksachi Lodge is open year-round.

Access Overview

Although Sequoia National Park encompasses a good chunk of the rugged Sierra Nevada Mountains, the more developed areas of the park are substantially lower and offer a number of accessible trails and attractions. The back country sites have peaks over 14,000 feet high; however the lowest areas of the Foothill section of the park are about 1,300 feet high, while the Giant Forest and Lodgepole areas have elevations around 6,000 feet. That said, the elevation can change quickly along the park roads, so it's important to make note of it if you may be susceptible to altitude sickness.

There are four free shuttle bus routes through the park during the summer

The Sentinel Tree at the Giant Forest Musem

months. The buses take visitors to the Giant Forest, Crescent Meadow, Lodgepole, Wuksachi Lodge, the General Sherman Tree and Wolverton Picnic Area. All of the park shuttle buses are wheelchair-accessible, kneel, and are equipped with ramps and wheelchair tie-downs.

The Giant Forest Museum makes a good first stop as it offers a comprehensive overview of the forest ecosystem. There's barrier-free access to the museum, that's housed in the former Giant Forest Market which was built in 1928. The museum includes a ranger information station, a small gift shop, and wheelchair-height exhibits about the Giant Forest. A manual wheelchair is available for loan at the front desk, and accessible restrooms are located near the gift shop.

The Sentinel Tree, which is a "typical Sequoia" is located directly in front of the museum – you can't miss it. There's a measuring tape painted on the asphalt pathway near the tree, that illustrates the height of this giant. This is probably the most accessible sequoia in the Giant Forest, as it's close enough to the museum for everyone to enjoy.

The General Sherman Tree, which is located a short drive from the museum, can be accessed from the lower parking lot via a quarter-mile paved trail. Accessible parking is available in the lower lot, and the shuttle bus also stops there in the summer. The upper parking lot for the General Sherman Tree is located a half-mile from the accessible lot, off of Wolverton

Start of the Big Trees Trail

Road. Although there's also accessible parking in this lot, the trail that leads down to the General Sherman tree is steep, has many sets of steps, and is not accessible. Although it's just a half-mile down to the tree, there is a 212-foot elevation change; and even though some slow walkers may be able to manage the downhill trek, it's important to note that the shuttle that takes visitors back to the upper lot only runs in the summer. And if you can't manage the entire length of the trail from the lower lot, you can still get an excellent view of the towering giant about .1-mile up the trail

Finally, make sure and check out the Big Trees Trail, which offers an accessible trek through the giant sequoia grove in Round Meadow. The accessible parking lot for the trail is located near the trailhead, just north of the Giant Forest Museum. From there the 2/3-mile loop trail begins as a wide paved path, before it transitions to an accessible boardwalk when it reaches the wetlands area. Interpretive plaques are located along the way, and it's not unusual to see bear and deer in the meadow.

The Tunnel Log in Sequoia National Park

Don't Miss This

Although the highlight of Sequoia National Park is the Giant Forest, plan for an early morning excursion to Crescent Meadow to enjoy another aspect of the park. The road to Moro Rock and Crescent Meadow is located next to the Giant Forest Museum; and although it's closed to private vehicles on the weekends and holidays; visitors with accessible parking placards can drive along it at any time.

The Auto Log is the first stop along the route. This fallen sequoia once had an asphalt driveway that enabled vehicles to drive up on the log. The massive tree — which has a 21-foot diameter — fell 1917; and after the driveway was constructed it was all the rage to have your vehicle photographed on the log. Today it's not possible to drive on the log, but it's still a fun stop to see the remnants of this former attraction. There's a small paved lot, but it's not striped, so it's best to park parallel if you have a ramp or lift. From the parking area, it's easy to roll on over to the log and read the interpretive plaque.

Just up the road you'll find the equally impressive Tunnel Log. Unlike the Auto Log, you can actually still drive trough this log; in fact, it's the only tree in the park that you can drive through. Rest assured though, there is a bypass if you have a large vehicle. The tunnel was created by the Civilian

Beginning of the Crescent Meadow Trail

Conservation Corp (CCC) after this 275-foot tree fell in the middle of the road in 1937. There's no official parking lot, but there's a large paved pullout on the right, with level access over to an interpretive sign. And then of course, you can drive through the log.

The road culminates at Crescent Meadow, which offers a scenic trail that may be doable for some folks. The paved trail continues for about a quarter-mile before it crosses a bridge and then heads uphill. Manual wheelchair-users will need some assistance on the first uphill grade, but if you make it past this obstacle you're good to go. The first view of Crescent Meadow — dubbed as "the gem of the Sierra" by John Muir — is just around the corner. A paved level area offers a panoramic overview of this magnificent meadow; and if you hit the trail early in the morning you may even see some bears foraging for food there. It's definitely worth the short uphill trek. From there, the paved trail continues along the meadow for another quarter-mile before it loses its access, however the one-mile round-trip hike is still quite enjoyable.

Insider Tip

Located on the west side of Generals Highway, just north of the Foothills Visitor Center, Tunnel Rock is definitely worth a stop – however the access

Tunnel Rock on Generals Highway

depends on where you park. The tunnel, which was once part of the old road, was crafted by CCC workers in 1930, when they dug beneath a big boulder to create a vehicle passageway along the road. Cars can no longer drive through the tunnel, but visitors can stop and have a look at this vestige from yesteryear, complete with a section of the old road.

For best access, visit this roadside stop as you head south, as there's accessible parking with curb-cut access just north of the tunnel on the west side of the road. There's barrier-free access from the parking space along a sidewalk, to the old road that passes through the small tunnel. Interestingly enough, there's evidence of where vehicles just literally scraped by on the roof of the tunnel, which is perhaps why the new road was built. It should be noted that the pullout on the south side of the tunnel is not accessible, and even dangerous with the heavy traffic; so resist the urge to stop while headed north.

Resources

Sequoia National Park
(559) 565-3341
www.nps.gov/seki
www.facebook.com/SequoiaKingsNPS
twitter.com/@sequoiakingsnps

Sequoia National Park Road Conditions
(559) 565-3341, then press 1

Sierra National Forest Road Conditions
CalTrans
(800) 427-7623

Delaware North (NPS Concessionaire)
(866) 807-3598
www.visitsequoia.com
Wuksachi Lodge

Barrier-Free Travel; Yosemite, Sequoia and Kings Canyon National Parks for Wheelers and Slow Walkers
www.barrierfreeyosemite.com

Yosemite National Park

Set aside as a national park in 1890, Yosemite includes over 1,200 square miles of scenic beauty in the rugged Sierra Nevada Mountains. And although the park boasts a large wilderness area, the bulk of the visitors gravitate to Yosemite Valley, where there's a good offering of accessible services, attractions and overnight accommodations.

There are five entrance stations to the park, four of which allow access to Yosemite Valley. The Big Oak Flat Entrance is located a half-hour east of Groveland, on Highway 120. This is the closest entrance for visitors from the San Francisco Bay Area. The Arch Rock Entrance is located a hour east of Mariposa on Highway 140. The South Entrance is located on Highway 41, about 30 minutes north of Oakhurst. This entrance is most often used by Southern California traffic. The Tioga Pass Entrance is located on the east side of the park, about 35 minutes north of Mammoth Lakes off Highway 395.

Additionally the Hetch Hetchy Entrance is located about 20 minutes north of the Big Oak Flat Entrance on Evergreen Road. This is the only park entrance that does not lead to Yosemite Valley, but instead offers visitors access to the scenic drive to Hetch Hetchy Reservoir.

Yosemite National Park is open year-round, and the major roads in the valley are plowed in the winter. Visitors are advised to carry chains or cables, as they can be required at any time from November to May. Yosemite Valley may also close during periods of extreme rainfall, as parts of the valley are prone to flooding.

Tioga Road usually closes from November to May, but depending on weather conditions it can still be closed in late June. The road to Hetch Hetchy is also open all year; however it may be closed intermittently in the winter due to snow. And although Glacier Point Road is open to Badger Pass in the winter, the remainder of the road is usually closed from November to May.

There are four lodges in Yosemite National Park, three of which have wheelchair-accessible rooms.

Admission

$35 – seven-day pass
$70 – yearly pass

Spend the Night
The Ahwahnee

1 Ahwahnee Drive
Yosemite National Park, CA 95389
(888) 413-8869
www.travelyosemite.com

Known as the crown jewel of Yosemite National Park, The Ahwahnee dates back to the 1920s. Open year-round, it's the site of presidential visits, fairy tale weddings and grand holiday celebrations. The architecture is a subtle mix of Art Deco, Native American and Middle Eastern styles; and the towering ceilings, stained glass windows and a massive stone fireplace serve to unite these cultures and present a welcoming — and distinctly mountain — venue. And if that's not enough, this upscale property also offers impressive views of Half Dome, Glacier Point and Yosemite Falls.

Accessible parking is available near the entrance, with level access to the front lobby. Complimentary valet parking is also offered; and if you need a little help getting around the grounds, a loaner wheelchair is available at the concierge desk.

The Ahwahnee in Yosemite National Park

Room 421 in the Ahwahnee

The view from room 421 in the Ahwahnee

Bathroom in room 421 in the Ahwahnee

The property features three types of wheelchair-accessible rooms — hotel rooms, junior suites and cottage rooms.

Room 421 is an accessible hotel room. It's furnished with a 27-inch high king-sized bed with wheelchair access on both sides, an armoire, an easy chair and a mini refrigerator.

The bathroom is equipped with a roll-in shower with grab bars, a hand-held showerhead and a fold-down shower bench. Toilet grab bars are located on the back and right walls (as seated), and there's also a roll-under sink in the bathroom.

And although this is just a standard hotel room, it also boasts one of the best views of Half Dome in the park.

Room 116 is also an accessible hotel room. It's furnished with a double bed and equipped with a roll-in shower.

Room 206, which was added to the inventory in 2016, is an accessible junior suite. Access features include wide doorways, barrier-free pathways, and plenty of room to wheel around this spacious suite, which occupies the space of two standard hotel rooms.

The sitting room has a 12-inch high single sofa bed, two end tables, a coffee table, two side chairs, an armoire and a mini refrigerator. There's level access to the adjacent bedroom, which features equally good access, and is furnished with a 30-inch high king-sized bed with wheelchair-access on both sides, two bedside tables, a small table with two chairs, an armoire and a mini refrigerator.

Room 206 in the Ahwahnee

The bathroom has a full five-foot turning radius, and is equipped with a roll-in shower with grab bars, a hand-held showerhead and a fold-down shower bench. The toilet grab bars are located on the back and left walls (as seated), and the bathroom also has a roll-under sink.

Sitting room in room 206 in the Ahwahnee

Bathroom in room 206 in the Ahwahnee

Top it off with a lowered peephole, lever handles and a lowered clothing rod, and you have a very well designed and functional accessible room.

Room 106 is also an accessible junior suite, but the bathroom is equipped with a tub/shower combination.

The accessible duplex cottages are located a short walk from the main lodge, along a level dogwood-lined path. Cottage 703 features barrier-free access to the front door, as well as the adjacent cement patio that's furnished with a table and three chairs. Inside, there's good pathway access throughout the cottage, which is furnished with two 27-inch high double beds with wheelchair access on the right sides (as you face them). Other furnishings include a bedside table, a table and two chairs, a chest of drawers, a desk with a chair, and a mini refrigerator.

The bathroom is equipped with a roll-in shower with grab bars, a hand-held showerhead and a fold-down shower bench. The toilet grab bars are located on the back and right walls (as seated), and there's a roll-under sink in the bathroom. There's also a barrier-free pathway to the closet and vanity area, which is located across the hall from the bathroom.

Cottage 702 has the same access features as cottage 703, except that it's furnished with a king-sized bed. And if you're traveling with family or an attendant, there's a connecting door between the two accessible cottages.

Cottage 703 at the Ahwahnee

There's good access to the public areas of the hotel as well, including the lobby, gift shop, lounge and dining room. Accessible family restrooms are located on the lobby level (men's), and on the mezzanine (women's), with elevator access to the upper floors. And thanks to some recent access

Bedroom in cottage 703 at the Ahwahnee

Bathroom in cottage 703 at the Ahwahnee

improvements, there's also elevator access to the upper floors from the solarium. Additionally there's level access out to the back lawn (a favorite wedding site), to the lift-equipped pool and around the cottages.

And although access features have been added over the years to this historic property, it still retains the charm — and look — of yesteryear.

The Ahwahnee is open year-round.

Yosemite Valley Lodge

9006 Yosemite Lodge Drive
Yosemite National Park, CA 95389
(888) 413-8869
www.travelyosemite.com

Located across the street from Yosemite Falls, this year-round lodge is a good choice for families, groups and even couples. The guestrooms are located in buildings that surround the main lobby building; and they offer good views of the adjacent forest through large windows and sliding glass doors.

The 245-room property has 10 wheelchair-accessible rooms, all of which have roll-in showers and queen-sized beds. There's accessible parking in front of the lodge, with ramp access up to the main lobby on the right side. Inside, there's barrier-free access through the lobby, over to the lowered front desk. Accessible restrooms are located around the corner, and there's a lowered pay phone near the accessible back entrance.

Room 4501 is located a short walk from the lobby, with accessible parking

Room 4501 at the Yosemite Valley Lodge

available in a nearby parking lot. Access features include wide doorways, good pathway access, lever handles and a lowered clothing rod.

The room is furnished with a 25-inch high queen-sized bed with

Bathroom in room 4501 at the Yosemite Valley Lodge

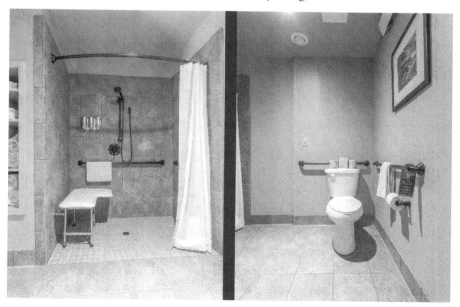

wheelchair access on both sides, a table with two chairs, a chest of drawers and a mini refrigerator. A sliding glass door allows level access out to a cement patio that's furnished with a table and two chairs. It's a pleasant place to relax after a full day of sightseeing.

The spacious bathroom is equipped with a roll-in shower with grab bars, a hand-held showerhead and a fold-down padded shower bench. The toilet grab bars are located on the back and left walls (as seated), and a roll-under sink is just outside the bathroom. Add in a full five-foot turning radius, and shower controls that are within easy reach of the shower bench, and you have a very accessible guestroom.

There's good access to all the public areas of the property, including the gift shop which is located across from the lobby, and the amphitheater which is situated in an alcove between the restaurants and the lobby. The amphitheater features bench seating on a cement surface, with designated wheelchair spaces located next to the benches. There's also barrier-free access to the Mountain Room and adjacent lounge, which are open in the evening; as well as the cafeteria-style Base Camp Eatery which is open all day.

Yosemite Valley Lodge is open year-round.

Curry Village

9010 Curry Village Drive
Yosemite National Park, CA 95389
(888) 413-8869
www.travelyosemite.com

Curry Village (formerly Camp Curry) played an important role in the development of California's first national park; in fact, the property has been welcoming guests to its tented cabins since 1899 — when Yosemite Valley was still a state park. Today the original log-crafted Camp Curry sign still graces the entrance, as a salute to this historic property.

Accessible parking is located near the front office, with level access to the historic building through the front door. Curry Village has five types of accessible accommodations — wooden cabins with a bathroom, wooden cabins without a bathroom, tent cabins, a historic lodge room and a specialty cabin.

Cabin 3B is an accessible wooden cabin with a bathroom. There's accessible parking in the lot in front of the cabin, with ramp access up to the front door. Access features include a wide front door with a level threshold, good pathway access and a lowered clothing rod.

Duplex cabin 3B in Curry Village

The cabin is furnished with a twin and full bed (both 26 inches high), with an access aisle between them. The full bed also has wheelchair-access on the left side as you face it. Other furnishings in this simple cabin include a chest of drawers and a chair.

Bedroom in cabin 3B in Curry Village

Bathroom in cabin 3B in Curry Village

The bathroom is equipped with a roll-in shower with grab bars, a hand-held showerhead and a fold-down shower bench. The toilet grab bars are located on the back and right walls (as seated), and there's also a roll-under sink in the spacious bathroom.

Cabin 2A has the same configuration and accessibility as cabin 3B.

Accessible cabin 1114 features ramp access to the front door. The cabin is located a short walk from an accessible parking space, but golf cart

Cabin 1114 in Curry Village

Inside cabin 1114 in Curry Village

transportation is available for folks who can't manage the distance. This basic cabin is furnished with two 24-inch high double beds with an access aisle between them, a bedside table, a chest of drawers, and a chair.

500's bathhouse in Curry Village

Inside the 500's bathhouse in Curry Village

There's no bathroom in cabin 1114, but the "500's bathhouse" — which is along the most accessible path of travel — is located about halfway between the cabin and the parking lot. It features ramp access on one end, and barrier-free access to a private accessible bathroom that's equipped with a roll-in shower with grab bars, a hand-held showerhead, a fold-down shower bench, and a plastic shower bench. Other access features include toilet grab bars on the back and right walls (as seated), and a roll-under sink. This accessible bathroom is kept locked to prevent misuse, but the key is available to disabled guests at the front office.

Accessible tent cabin 7 also lacks a bathroom, but it features level access and a wide door. It's furnished with a 21-inch high full and twin bed, with an access aisle between them. It also includes a heater (very necessary in the winter), and a bear box outside the front door. And although there's no parking in front of the cabin, guests with an accessible parking placard can drive up to the tent cabin on the service road to drop off passengers and gear.

The closest accessible bathhouse to cabin 7 is located near the swimming pool, just a short walk from the front office. This bathhouse features level access on both the men's and women's sides, with ample room to navigate a wheelchair inside. Both sides are equipped with an accessible toilet stall, roll-under sinks and a large (double-sized) roll-in shower with grab bars and a hand-held showerhead. A plastic shower chair and a shower bench are also provided; and even with both chairs in the shower area, there's still plenty of room for even a large wheelchair or scooter. There's also barrier-free access to the locker area.

Tent cabin 7

Tent cabins 6, 9, 215, 217, 218 and 219 have the same configuration and accessibility as tent cabin 7.

There's one accessible hotel room in the historic Stoneman Cottage, located

Inside tent cabin 7

Bedroom in Stoneman Cottage room 810

next door to the front office. Although there are a few steps up to the Stoneman building from the office side, there's level access to accessible room 810 from the accessible parking area on the opposite side. There is also a barrier-free pathway from this room to the dining pavilion.

This spacious corner room is furnished with a 28-inch high double bed with wheelchair access on both sides, a bedside table, a chest of drawers, and an easy chair.

Bathroom in Stoneman Cottage room 810

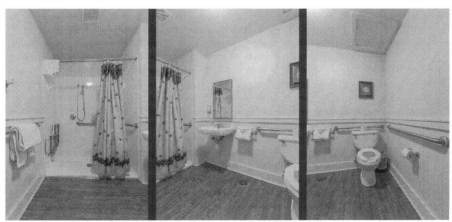

The bathroom features a full five-foot turning radius, and is equipped with a roll-in shower with grab bars, a hand-held showerhead and a fold-down shower bench. The toilet grab bars are located on the back and left walls (as seated), and the bathroom also has a roll-under sink. A portable shower chair is available upon request for this — or any — room at Curry Village.

Specialty cabin 819 is also an excellent choice for wheelchair-users and slow walkers. This one-of-a-kind historic cabin, which was once Mother Curry's home, was renovated in 2018 to be wheelchair-accessible. And they did an excellent job.

The cabin is located near the office, and there's an accessible pathway from both the office and the nearby accessible parking area to the front door of the cabin. Access features include level access to the front porch, wide doorways, low-pile carpet and good pathway access inside.

The living area is furnished with a table and two chairs, a 13-inch high sleeper sofa, a coffee table, and two easy chairs. A large fireplace occupies the bulk of one wall, and there's also a good supply of firewood on the hearth. Additionally, there's a small refrigerator in the living area — a coveted feature in the national park.

The bedroom is furnished with a 27-inch high king-sized bed with wheelchair access on the right side (as you face it), some night tables and a

Specialty cabin 819

Living area in specialty cabin 819

chest of drawers. The bathroom is equipped with a large roll-in shower with grab bars, a hand-held showerhead and a fold-down shower bench. The toilet grab bars are located on the back and left walls (as seated), and there's also a roll-under sink in the bathroom. It's a very roomy cottage, that's close

Bedroom in specialty cabin 819

Bathroom in specialty cabin 819

to the public facilities, with access features that everyone can appreciate. It's also a great family option.

There's good access to the public areas of Curry Village as well. The amphitheater, which is located near the tent cabins, features level access and room for wheelchair seating on the sides and in front. The historic Lounge, which is located next door, offers level access on the left side, and wide doors with level thresholds. Inside, the walls are dotted with vintage photographs, and there's comfy seating around the stone fireplace, with private nooks to work or read. There is also level access to the dining areas next door; and if you just want to explore the property and enjoy the outdoors, there are a number of level pathways throughout the large complex.

Curry Village operates seven days a week from March to the end of November, and from mid-December to January 1. It's closed from the end of November to mid-December; and open on weekends only from January to March.

Access Overview

Numerous access upgrades have been made to Yosemite National Park over the years, which have substantially increased the access at Yosemite Falls, Glacier Point, Mariposa Grove and many of the park lodges. The park has a wide range of elevations; from just under 2,000 feet near the Arch Rock Entrance, to 13,144 feet at the summit of Mount Lyell. The highest point navigable by vehicle is Tioga Pass, which logs in at an impressive 9,945 feet. That said, Yosemite Valley – the most popular stop for visitors — has a elevation of just 4,000 feet.

One of the great things about Yosemite is that you don't need a vehicle to get around – or even to – the park. The Yosemite Area Regional Transportation System (YARTS) provides fixed route public transportation to Yosemite from Merced, Fresno, Mammoth Lakes and Sonora. All YARTS buses are wheelchair-accessible; however passengers that require wheelchair seating must contact YARTS at least 48 hours in advance to insure availability.

Although vehicle traffic is still allowed in most areas of the valley, the Yosemite Valley shuttle is the easiest way to get around the park. All of the shuttle buses are wheelchair-accessible, and they stop at the lodges, stores, trailheads and major vistas in the valley. Best of all, there's no charge to ride the shuttle.

And if you'd like a more in-depth tour of the park, then hop on one of Aramark's classic valley floor tours. These two-hour naturalist-led tours introduce visitors to the highlights of Yosemite, and present a good primer on the natural history of the park. During good weather the tours are conducted in open-air trams which offer a magnificent view of the surrounding natural features; but in inclement weather, buses replace the trams. Accessible tour vehicles are available with 48 hours advance notice.

Yosemite Falls

One of the most accessible hikes in the valley is the east trail to Lower Yosemite Fall. Completed in 2005, this wide paved trail leads through the forest to the base of Lower Yosemite Fall. A short boardwalk section of the trail covers a muddy stretch, and has low bumpers for unobstructed wheelchair viewing. There are benches and interpretive plaques along the way, and it's a pleasant spot to just sit back and enjoy Mother Nature.

Mirror Lake is also worth a stop; and although vehicles are prohibited along the Mirror Lake Road, visitors with an accessible parking placard are allowed to drive on it. Temporary accessible parking placards are also available at all entrance stations and visitor centers in the park, for visitors who are temporarily disabled, or who do not have their placard with them. Mirror Lake is a nice spot for a picnic, as some of the picnic tables are on level ground. It should be noted that the lake itself is seasonal, and it usually dries up by late summer; however the site always boasts some spectacular granite views. Be sure and check out the Happy Isles Nature Trail on the way back. This scenic stroll travel along the Merced River makes a nice .8-mile loop. The trail is hard-packed dirt, level and fairly free of debris during the dry months.

Located at 7,214 feet, Glacier Point is the best spot to get a commanding view of Yosemite Valley. There's barrier-free access out to the lower viewpoint and the amphitheater — a favorite wedding venue — with accessible seating available in the back row of the amphitheater. Although

Happy Isles Nature Trail

Hetch Hetchy Reservoir in Hetch Hetchy Valley

the path out to the upper viewpoint is steep and has stairs along the way, there's an accessible path just to the left of the stairs. This wide paved pathway features a number of switchbacks and offers a gentle — and accessible — climb to the upper viewpoint. Signage is also good at Glacier Point, so it's relatively easy to locate the accessible route.

Finally, if you'd like to ditch the crowds for a day, take the scenic drive to Hetch Hetchy Valley. The road travels through gray pine, incense cedar and black oak forests, and features some breathtaking windshield views across the canyon. As an added bonus, you can catch glimpses of Hetch Hetchy Reservoir from almost the beginning of the road.

Don't Miss This

Most people never make it out of Yosemite Valley, and totally miss the incredible scenery along Tioga Road, which connects Crane Flat on the west with Highway 395 on the east. The 39-mile road transitions from forests and meadows to lakes and granite domes, before it crosses Tioga Pass at the 9,945 foot elevation point. Make sure and stop at the east end of Tenaya Lake, as an accessible path leads .1-mile out to the lakeshore, where there's a secluded accessible picnic table. It's a pleasant spot to enjoy the view, even if you don't stop for lunch.

Insider Tip

The newly renovated Mariposa Grove, which is located near the South Entrance, is definitely worth a stop; however many visitors totally miss it in their rush to see the valley attractions. Although shuttle service to the grove is mandatory, visitors with accessible parking placards can drive to the grove and park at the Mariposa Grove Arrival Center or in the Grizzly Giant parking area.

From the Mariposa Grove Arrival Center, the .3-mile Big Trees Loop leads through the grove of giant sequoias. Although the trail loops back around to the parking lot, there is a short accessible jag out to the Fallen Monarch — a sequoia that came down more than 300 years ago — midway along the trail. Even if you can't do the whole loop, take some time to enjoy the sequoia forest on the boardwalk near the beginning of the trail.

The Grizzly Giant Loop, which can be accessed from the second parking area, passes the massive Grizzly Giant as well as the the iconic California Tunnel Tree. The 2/3-mile round-trip hike winds through the forest over undulating hard-packed dirt trails. It's a pleasant accessible stroll, but get there early in the day for a more serene experience, as the grove tends to get crowded after mid-morning.

California Tunnel Tree on the Grizzly Giant Loop trail at Mariposa Grove

Resources

Yosemite National Park
(209) 372-0200
www.nps.gov/yose
www.facebook.com/YosemiteNPS
twitter.com/YosemiteNPS

Yosemite Accessibility Coordinator
(209) 379-1035
yose_accessibility@nps.gov

Yosemite Road Conditions
(209) 372-0200, then press 1

YARTS
(877) 989-2787

Aramark (NPS Concessionaire)
(888) 413-8869
www.travelyosemite.com
The Ahwahnee
Yosemite Valley Lodge
Curry Village

Barrier-Free Travel; Yosemite, Sequoia and Kings Canyon National Parks for Wheelers and Slow Walkers
www.barrierfreeyosemite.com

Colorado

Square Tower House in Mesa Verde National Park

Mesa Verde National Park

Established in 1906, Mesa Verde National Park was home to the Ancestral Pueblo people, some 700 years ago. These mysterious inhabitants disappeared without a trace, but left evidence of their existence, with the 5,000 archaeological sites and 600 cliff dwellings that are scattered throughout this Southwestern Colorado site. And although cliff dwellings are far from accessible, wheelchair-users and slow walkers can still get a good gander at them from many of the accessible viewpoints in the park.

The entrance to Mesa Verde National Park is located off of Highway 160, about ten miles southeast of Cortez, Colorado.

The main park road is open year-round, however snow or ice may close it temporarily in the winter. Mesa Top Loop is also open year-round, weather permitting; however it's only open during the days in the winter months. After the first snowfall, the Cliff Palace Loop is closed; and Weatherhill Mesa Road is only open from May through September. Conditions can change quickly, so visitors are advised to carry chains or cables.

There is one lodge in Mesa Verde National Park.

Admission

$15 – seven-day pass (January – April and November – December)

$25 – seven day pass (May – October)

$50 – yearly pass

Spend the Night
Far View Lodge

Mile Marker 15
Mesa Verde National Park, CO 81330
(800) 449-2288
www.visitmesaverde.com

Located about a mile north of the Far View Sites, this 150-room seasonal property features good access and great views of the surrounding countryside.

There's accessible parking near the main lodge building, with level access to the lobby. From there it's just a short drive to accessible room 159. There's no striped parking in front of the room, but the lot is paved and there's plenty of space to pull up right outside the room.

Access features include a threshold ramp, wide doorways, a lowered clothing rod and good pathway access throughout the room. Decorated in a western theme, the room is furnished with a 22-inch high queen-sized bed with wheelchair access on both sides, a chest of drawers, a desk and a refrigerator.

Room 159 at Far View Lodge

Bathroom in room 159 at Far View Lodge

The spacious bathroom is equipped with a 36-inch-square transfer-type shower with a fold-down shower bench, grab bars and a handheld showerhead. The toilet grab bars are located on the back and right walls (as seated), and a roll-under sink is located just outside the bathroom. The bathroom is very nicely done, and it even includes lowered towel bars.

One of the best features of this room is the private balcony, which features level access and plenty of room for a wheelchair. Even if it's too cold to sit outside, you can still enjoy the view through the large picture window. And since there's no television in the room, you can occupy your time by star gazing and enjoying all that Mother Nature has to offer — and that's reason enough make Far View Lodge your home base in Mesa Verde National Park.

There's barrier-free access to the public areas of the property as well, including the Far View Terrace Cafe, which serves casual fare and is open for breakfast, lunch and dinner. The Mesa Mocha Espresso Bar is also wheelchair-accessible, and it offers grab-and-go breakfasts and lunches as well as coffee drinks in the mornings.

Far view Lodge is open from mid-April to late October.

Access Overview

Although much of this national park is located in rugged terrain, a good number of the archaeological sites can be viewed from accessible viewpoints along Mesa Top Loop. That said, elevations in the park range from 7,000 feet to 8,500 feet, so take it slow and remember to drink a lot of water.

This scenic six-mile Mesa Top Loop drive features a variety of archaeological sites grouped in chronological order, and offers a good representation of the variety of housing styles used by the Ancestral Pueblo people. Recommended stops include the first pithouse, the pithouses and pueblos site, and the first, second and third mesa top villages. All of the sites feature accessible parking and have a paved trail to the ruins. Most of the sites are located near the road, and many of the ruins are covered. Additionally, you can get a good windshield view of the Oak Tree House cliff dwelling from up on Mesa Top Loop.

There are several overlooks along the main park road that also merit a stop, including Montezuma Valley, Mancos Valley, Geologic and Park Point. Although these stops may not include access features, most are doable with a little assistance.

The Chapin Mesa Archeological Museum also has some doable access. Although there are several groups of steps throughout this historic building,

Pithouse along the Mesa Top Loop

the rangers are happy to set up portable ramps for folks who cannot manage them. This museum presents a comprehensive history of the Ancestral Pueblo people, and includes artifacts that were excavated in the park.

And although Weatherhill Mesa Road makes a scenic drive, most of the sites have steps and ladders and they are not wheelchair-accessible.

Don't Miss This

Make sure and stop at the Far View Sites, located about three miles north of Spruce Tree House on Chapin Mesa Road. At one time this area was the most densely populated spot on the mesa, with as many as 50 villages. Today the pueblo style ruins are scattered throughout the area.

Unfortunately, uneven terrain prevents accessible travel to all of the ruins, but the Far View House is doable for most folks. It's located close to the level dirt parking area; and although the dirt trail around the site has some access obstacles, most folks will be able to navigate the first part. Some slow walkers may also be able to access the entire 3/4-mile dirt trail to all the ruins, so give it a try if it looks doable. Even if you've had your fill of walking, you can still get a good view of the ruins from your car, so don't miss this stop.

Ruins at Far View Sites

Insider Tip

Although the Spruce Tree House — one of the major cliff dwellings in the park — is closed for a geotechnical assessment, you can still get a good view of it, if you know where to go. Some overlooks near the Chapin Mesa Archaeological Museum offer a decent view, but the best vantage point is located in the level area behind the Chief Ranger's Office next to the Chapin Mesa Archeological Museum. Don't forget to bring your binoculars for a close-up look at the details of this archaeological ruin.

Resources

Mesa Verde National Park
(970) 529-4465
www.nps.gov/meve
www.facebook.com/mesaverdenps

Road Conditions
(970) 529-4465

Aramark (NPS Concessionaire)
(800) 449-2288
www.visitmesaverde.com
Far View Lodge

Kentucky

Sloan's Crossing Pond Walk in Mammoth Cave National Park

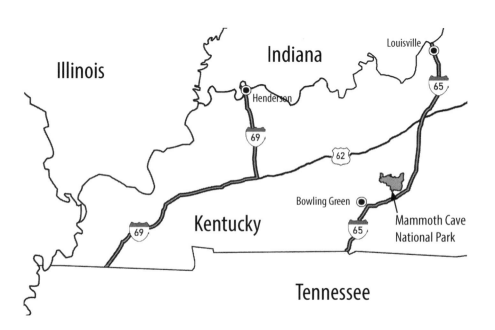

Mammoth Cave National Park

Located 90 miles south of Louisville, Mammoth Cave National Park is named for the enormous 412-mile long cave that runs under the park. The subterranean wonders however, are just part of this park's draw; as visitors are also wowed by the scenic river valleys of over 50,000 acres of Kentucky hill country. And although caves are usually not accessible by their very nature, the recent addition of an elevator makes Mammoth Cave an exception. Add in a gaggle of accessible trails, and you have a full dance card for wheelers and slow walkers.

There are numerous entrances to Mammoth Cave National Park, but these main access points lead to the areas of the park that have the most visitor services.

The south park entrances are located off Interstate 65, at exit 48 near Park City, and exit 53 in Cave City.

The west park entrance is located east of Brownsville off of Highway 70.

The east park entrance is located near exit 58 off of Interstate 65, east of Northtown.

The north entrance is located on Road 1352, which enters the park on Green River Ferry Road. This route requires a river crossing on the Green River Ferry, which suspends service when the water levels are too high or low. Check with the ferry hotline at (270) 758-2166 for updated schedule information. In the event of a ferry closure, the nearest entrance is on the west near Brownsville.

Keep in mind that GPS is not very accurate in the park, so it's best to stick to maps and road signs.

Mammoth Cave National Park is open year-round; however some park roads may be closed during severe weather.

There is one lodge in Mammoth Cave National Park.

Admission

There is no admission fee to Mammoth Cave National Park; however there is a charge for the cave tours.

Spend the Night

The Lodge at Mammoth Cave
717 Hotel Road
Mammoth Cave, KY 42259
(844) 760-2283
www.mammothcavelodge.com

You just can't beat the location of The Lodge at Mammoth Cave, as it's right behind the visitor center, and just steps from the accessible Heritage Trail. There's accessible parking near the office, with a barrier-free path over to the front door. Inside, there's plenty of room to maneuver a wheelchair over to the registration desk of this single-story property, which evokes memories of yesteryear.

The Lodge at Mammoth Cave has eight accessible rooms, six of which are equipped with a roll-in shower.

Room 400, which is a recently renovated accessible Heritage Trail Room, is located right around the corner from the front desk. It features wide doorways, low-pile carpet, lever handles, a lowered closet rod and good pathway access. Furnishings include two 27-inch high open-frame queen-sized beds, with wheelchair access in the middle and right side (as you face them), an easy chair, a chest of drawers, a desk with a chair and a

Room 400 at the Lodge at Mammoth Cave

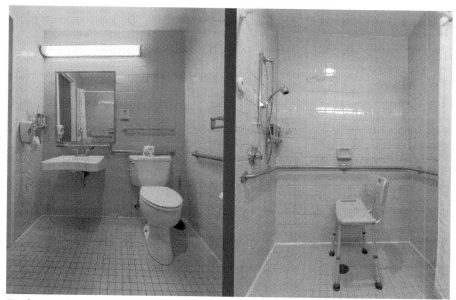

Bathroom in room 400 at the Lodge at Mammoth Cave

refrigerator. It also includes some coveted modern amenities, such as a phone, a television and even internet access.

The bathroom is equipped with a roll-in shower with grab bars, a hand-held showerhead and a portable shower chair. Other access features include toilet grab bars on the back and left walls (as seated), a roll-under sink and a lowered mirror.

Room 403 has the same access features as room 400.

There's also barrier-free access to all the public areas — including the Cave Gift Shop, the Green River Grill and Spelunkers Cafe — which are located off the main lobby. And if you'd like to take a stroll through the woods, the accessible Heritage Trail begins right out the back door.

It's a very accessible property, and it makes a comfortable home base for any Mammoth Cave National Park visit.

The Lodge at Mammoth Cave is open year-round.

Access Overview

The highlight of any Mammoth Cave visit is of course a cave tour, and thanks to recent access upgrades wheelchair-users and slow walkers can now enjoy the wonders down under. And with an average elevation of just 630 feet, and a number of accessible trails, the surface also offers a number of recreational opportunities for everyone.

The Heritage Trail is the closest trail to the visitor center. This three-quarter-mile trail begins as a wide level path, before it transitions to a newly redone boardwalk section that loops through the forest and offers good views of the park. Sunset Point, which is located mid-way along the trail, also offers some nice views. There is also a short 300-foot trail out to the Old Guides Cemetery from the Heritage Trail. The level trail leads over to a abandoned graveyard, where Stephen Bishop — a guide who died in 1857 — was laid to rest.

Sloan's Crossing Pond Walk, which is just a short drive away on Mammoth Cave Parkway, is also worth a visit. This .4-mile boardwalk around the shaded pond is wide and level, and it's dotted with accessible viewing platforms, benches and interpretive plaques. Even if you can't do the whole trail, there's an excellent pond view from the first overlook, which is just steps from the parking area.

The Heritage Trail at Mammoth Cave National Park

Last but not least. the Sand Cave Trail makes a good stop on the way in or out of the park at the Cave City entrance. The .1-mile boardwalk winds through the forest, and because of the low bumpers, there are some nice open views. The trail terminates at an overlook, which has a view of the Sand Cave rescue site; where Floyd Collins was trapped and ultimately died in 1925. In spite of Floyd's unfortunate fate, it's actually a pleasant little stroll.

Don't Miss This

Without a doubt, a cave tour is a must-do at Mammoth Cave. The two-hour Accessible Cave Tour begins at the visitor center, where participants then drive their own vehicles to the elevator on Cave City Road. There's accessible parking in the lot, and barrier-free access over to the elevator. The tour of this gypsum cave travels over level cement pathways and visits the Snowball Room, and includes portions of the Cleveland Avenue Tour and the Grand Avenue Tour. It can accommodate even large power wheelchairs and scooters, and it's a very manageable half-mile in length.

Some slow walkers may also be able to manage the Frozen Niagara Tour. This one-and-a-half-hour tour begins just outside the visitor center, and travels by bus to the cave entrance. There are 12 stairs down to the cave, and another 98 optional stairs along this fairly level tour.

Elevator to Mammoth Cave

No mater which tour you choose, be sure and get your tickets early. This is especially true for the Accessible Cave Tour as it's quite poplar. Tickets can be purchased online at www.recreation.gov, or by calling the National Park Reservation Service at (877) 444-6777. Half of the tickets are available for advance purchase, while the other half are available on the day of the tour.

Insider Tip

The newest accessible trail in the park — the Echo River Spring Trail — isn't even noted on the park maps yet. The trailhead is located near the end of Green River Road. Accessible parking is available near the trailhead, and there's also an accessible porta-potty and an accessible picnic table near the parking lot. This one-mile trail begins as a wide cement walkway, before it transitions to a short boardwalk through the forest. At the .4-mile point it becomes a fairly level hard-packed dirt trail, before it ends at River Styx Spring. It's a pleasant stroll, and there are several overlooks with benches to sit back and enjoy the peaceful forest. As an added bonus, this is one of the least crowded areas of the park.

The Echo River Spring Trail in Mammoth Caves National Park

Resources

Mammoth Cave National Park
(270) 758-2180
www.nps.gov/maca
www.facebook.com/MammothCaveNPS
twitter.com/MammothCaveNP

Road Conditions
(270) 758-2180

Green River Ferry Hotline
(270) 758-2166

Cave Tours
(877) 444-6777
www.recreation.gov

Ortega National Parks (NPS Concessionaire)
(844) 760-2283
www.mammothcavelodge.com
www.facebook.com/MammothCaveLodge/
The Lodge at Mammoth Cave

Michigan

Rock Harbor Lighthouse in Isle Royale National Park

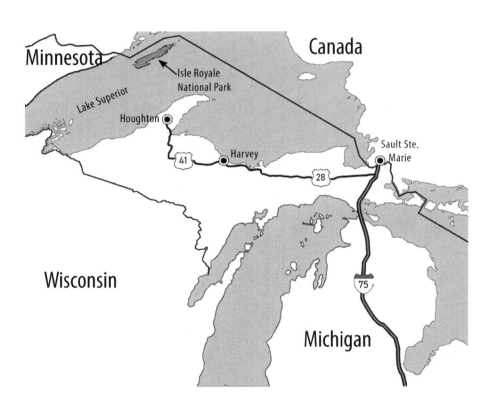

accessible family restroom, one that's comparable to the spacious models found on modern cruise ships.

Over at Rock Harbor, the boarding procedure is reversed, and there's ramp access down to the dock, and level access to the adjacent visitor center and general store. And since the highest point in the park is just 1,394 feet — and that's in the back country — there are no worries about altitude sickness in this national park.

Even though a good chunk of the park is not accessible, you just can't beat the views from the lodge. Additionally, there's ramp access to the Rock Harbor Auditorium, which offers nightly ranger programs about one of America's least visited national parks.

Don't Miss This

Don't be dissuaded by the shortage of accessible trails at Isle Royale National Park, as you don't have to go far to get up-close-and-personal with the abundant wildlife that inhabits the island. The paved level trail that runs from the dock to the lodge is an excellent wildlife viewing venue, so spend some time there, especially near dusk and dawn. The resident moose are known to frequent this area, and it's also a lovely place to enjoy the sunset.

Rock Harbor view

Insider Tip

Although the July 4 holiday is usually crowded at most national parks, that's not the case at Isle Royale. According to the *Ranger III* purser, Independence Day is an excellent time to visit the park, as most folks celebrate it on the mainland. Conversely, the first crossing after Labor Day is usually pretty crowded, as it's the last hurrah before ferry service ends in mid-September.

Resources

Isle Royale National Park
(906)482-0984
www.nps.gov/isro
www.facebook.com/IsleRoyaleNPS

Forever Resorts (NPS Concessionaire)
(906) 337-4993
www.rockharborlodge.com
www.facebook.com/RockHarborLodge
Rock Harbor Lodge

Ranger III
(906) 482-0984
www.nps.gov/isro/planyourvisit/rangeriii-reservation-instructions.htm

Montana

Apgar Picnic Area on Lake McDonald in Glacier Naional Park

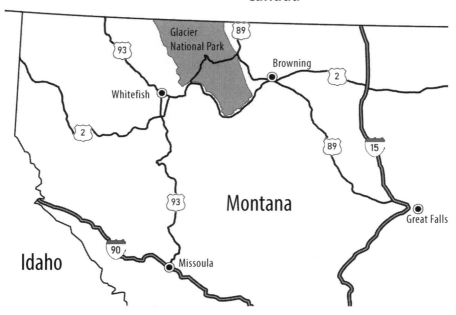

Glacier National Park

Known as the "Crown of the Continent" because the Continental Divide bisects it, Glacier National Park encompasses more than a million acres of coniferous forests, alpine meadows, pristine lakes and glacier-carved peaks. Located in Northwestern Montana, the park also supports a healthy population of elk, bighorn sheep, moose, and grizzly bears. Add in accessibility that parallels the park's diversity, with a nice selection of accessible tours, trails and attractions; and you have a very visitable national park.

There are four entrances to Glacier National Park.

The West Entrance is located 45 minutes northeast of Kalispell, 25 minutes northeast of Columbia Falls and 35 minutes northeast of Whitefish on Highway 2.

The St. Mary Entrance is located on the east side of the park, at the other end of the Going-to-the-Sun Road.

The Many Glacier Entrance is also located on the east side of the park, about a half-hour drive from the St. Mary Entrance.

The Two Medicine Entrance is in the southeast corner of the park, about 10 miles northwest of East Glacier.

Glacier National Park is open year-round; however the alpine portion of Going-to-the-Sun Road — which connects the east and west sections — is closed from late fall to late spring due to snow. Plowing this road is a massive undertaking, and portions of it open incrementally in the late spring as it's completed. The entire length of Going-to-the-Sun Road generally does not open until June or July, and it usually closes again in late October.

The portion of Going-to-the-Sun Road from West Glacier to Lake McDonald Lodge is maintained throughout the year; however other park roads may only be accessed by cross country skis or snowshoes during the winter.

There are six lodges with accessible rooms in the park; three are on the west side of the park, and three are on the east side.

Admission

$35 – seven-day pass (May 1 to October 31)
$25 – Seven day pass (November 1 to April 30)
$70 – yearly pass

Spend the Night

Village Inn at Apgar

Lake View Drive
West Glacier, MT 59936
(855) 733-4522
www.glaciernationalparklodges.com

Located on the shore of Lake McDonald, this motel-style property was built in 1956. And although the Americans with Disabilities Act didn't exist back then, access upgrades have been added to the property over the years. Today it offers two wheelchair-accessible rooms, with all the access features you expect find in a modern property. It's also in a great location — just two miles from the West Entrance of the park.

There's level access to the office, with accessible parking located on the far

Bedroom in room 60 at the Village Inn at Apgar

Sleeping area in room 60 at the Village Inn at Apgar

side, in front of accessible room 60. From there, it's a level roll to the front door of this comfy two-bedroom family unit. Inside, there's good pathway access, wide doorways, lever handles and low-pile carpet for easy rolling.

Kitchen in room 60 at the Village Inn at Apgar

This retro unit includes one bedroom that furnished with a 25-inch high queen-sized bed with wheelchair-access on the right side (as you face it), and two night stands. There's another sleeping area located in the front room, with a partial wall between it and the kitchen. It's furnished with a 20-inch high queen-sized bed with wheelchair access on both sides, and there are also two chairs on the far end of the room. And the best part about the placement of the bed, is that you can get a great lake view through the adjacent picture window.

The kitchen is outfitted with a stove, a refrigerator and a microwave; and there's a roll-under sink at the far end of the counter. A dining room table with four standard chairs is also included; and although one or two chairs may need to be moved for optimal wheelchair-access, it's really an easy fix. Add in the retro wall clock, and it's almost like you're back in the 1950s. There's nothing retro about the access in this room though!

The bathroom, which can be accessed through a wide pocket door, includes a full five-foot turning radius. It's equipped with a large roll-in shower with grab bars, a hand-held showerhead and a fold-down shower bench. Other access features include a toilet with grab bars on the back and right walls (as seated), and a roll-under sink.

By far, one of the best features of this room is the view — as the large picture window affords a panoramic peek at Lake Mc Donald. And if you'd like to get a closer look, there's level access out the back door, which leads to a

Bathroom in room 60 at the Village Inn at Apgar

Bedroom in room 95 at the Village Inn at Apgar

lakeside cement promenade furnished with Adirondack chairs.

Room 95, which is located at the far end of the complex, offers level access from the accessible parking space in front, to the wide back door along the

Bathroom in room 95 at the Village Inn at Apgar

lakeside promenade. This corner unit features the same basic access features as room 60, except that it's a bit smaller. It's furnished with a 25-inch high double bed with wheelchair-access on the left side (as you face it), and it includes a lowered wardrobe, a chair, and a small table.

There's level access to the oversized bathroom, which is furnished with a roll-in shower with grab bars, a hand-held showerhead, and a fold-down shower bench. Other access features include toilet grab bars on the back and left walls (as seated), a roll-under sink and a full five-foot turning radius.

This room also has the same great lake view as room 60.

And in keeping with the period in which the motel was constructed, none of the rooms at this property have a television, a telephone or air conditioning.

The Village Inn at Apgar is open from late May to early October.

Lake McDonald Lodge

288 Lake McDonald Loop
West Glacier, MT 59936
(855) 733-4522
www.glaciernationalparklodges.com

Lake McDonald Lodge

Located on the shore of Lake Mc Donald about 10 miles from West Glacier, this 1913 lodge features 82 guest rooms and cabins; and at first-glance the building evokes memories of a Swiss chalet. And in keeping with the ambience of an old time hunting lodge, there are no worldly distractions such as televisions or internet access at this property. Accessible parking is located near the main lobby, with ramp access down to the lobby level on the land side. Out in back — on the shore side — there's a gently sloping ramp that meanders down to the lakeshore, with picnic tables scattered nearby under the old growth trees.

This historic property has a variety of accessible rooms. Two accessible hotel rooms are located near the lobby on the first floor. One room is furnished with a queen-sized bed and has a bathroom that's equipped with a low-step shower with grab bars, a hand-held showerhead and a shower bench. The other room is furnished with a king-sized bed and includes a tub/shower combination with grab bars, a hand-held showerhead and a shower bench. Both rooms have ample space to maneuver a wheelchair.

There are also two accessible cabins on the property. They both feature ramp access, and include a bathroom with a low-step (four-inch) shower. One cabin is furnished with two double beds, and the other includes a king-sized bed. Both cabins feature ample room to maneuver a wheelchair.

Last but not least, there's an accessible hostel room located in historic

Historic Snyder Hall at Lake McDonald Lodge

Snyder Hall. Accessible parking is located behind the building, with a level path to the front door. The accessible room is located on the ground floor. It has ample room to maneuver a wheelchair and includes a double bed and a roll-under sink. The shared bathroom is located down the hall and is equipped with a tub/shower combination with a hand-held showerhead.

There's good wheelchair access to all the public areas of the lodge, including Russell's Fireside Dining Room, which offers portable ramp access and is open for breakfast, lunch and dinner.

Even if you don't stay at this property, make sure and stop by for a stroll around the beautiful grounds.

Lake McDonald Lodge is open from mid-May to late September.

Motel Lake McDonald

466 Lake McDonald Loop
West Glacier, MT 59936
(844) 868-7474
www.glacierparkinc.com

Located to the right of Lake McDonald Lodge, this 1950's style two-story motel offers rustic yet comfortable accommodations, just a stone's throw from picturesque Lake McDonald. Although there are steps up to the lobby,

Motel Lake McDonald

there is also level access from the accessible parking place on the side of the building. This property has one wheelchair-accessible room with a king-sized bed and a roll-in shower.

Motel Lake McDonald is open from early June to mid-September.

Rising Sun Motor Inn

Going-to-the-Sun Road
East Glacier Park, Mt 59434
(855) 733-4522
www.glaciernationalparklodges.com

Built in 1940, this 72-unit motel has seen some recent access upgrades. And it's very conveniently located, right across the street from the St. Mary Lake boat docks, and only six miles east of the St. Mary Entrance.

Accessible parking is located near the motel entrance, with ramp access up to the main building. Inside, there's barrier-free access through the small gift shop and over to the front desk. An accessible family restroom is located in the back of the gift shop.

All of the accessible rooms are located a short drive up the hill in the Upper Motel building. A newly constructed accessible parking area is located on a concrete pad, with a barrier-free path over to the building.

Room 27 at Rising Sun Motor Inn

Bathroom in room 27 at Rising Sun Motor Inn

Room 27 features wide doorways, good pathway access and a lowered clothing rod. It's furnished with a 25-inch high queen-sized bed with wheelchair access on both sides, an easy chair, two night tables and a desk with a chair.

The spacious bathroom features a full five-foot turning radius, and is equipped with a roll-in shower with grab bars, a hand-held showerhead and a fold-down shower bench. Other access features include toilet grab bars on the back and left walls (as seated), and a roll-under sink.

Bathroom in room 15 at Rising Sun Motor Inn

Room 26 has the same access features as room 27. Room 28 and room 15 are mirror images of room 27.

The rooms all have a few nostalgic touches, and in keeping with the era that the property was constructed, there are no televisions or telephones in the rooms.

There's also barrier-free access to Two Dog Flats Grill, which is located off the lobby. The classic American eatery offers breakfast favorites in the morning; and a nice selection of burgers, sandwiches, soups and salads, as well as fish, chicken and beef entrees for lunch and dinner.

The Rising Sun Motor Inn is open from mid-June to mid-September.

Many Glacier Hotel

36 Many Glacier Hotel Loop
Babb, MT 59411
(855) 733-4522
www.glaciernationalparklodges.com

Like Lake McDonald Lodge, the Many Glacier Hotel was built to resemble a Swiss chalet by the Great Northern Railway, in order to entice folks to visit the "American Alps". Accessible parking is located behind the main lodge building near the boat dock, with level access to the ground floor, and elevator access up to the lobby level. It should be noted that the day

Many Glacier Hotel on Lake McDonald

use parking area for the lodge is located up a series of stairways and hills, so it's best to use the large drop-off area in front of the lodge if you can't do distances or steps.

There's barrier-free access throughout the lobby level of the hotel, and all of the accessible rooms are located on this floor. The property has 12 accessible rooms, all of which have roll-in showers.

Room 114 features wide doorways and good pathway access, and is furnished with a double bed and twin bed (27-inches high), with wheelchair access on all sides. Other furnishings include an easy chair, and a desk with a chair. A second door leads out to a shared balcony which offers a great view of the lake. The back door has a 27-inch clearance, and there's room for a wheelchair or scooter on the large balcony.

The bathroom has a full five-foot turning radius, and is equipped with a roll-in shower with a slight one-inch lip, with grab bars, a hand-held showerhead and a fold-down shower bench. Other bathroom access features include toilet grab bars on the back and left walls (as seated), and a roll-under sink with a lowered mirror.

Room 102 features more floor space and is furnished with a 27-inch high queen-sized bed with wheelchair access on both sides. Other furnishings include an easy chair, a nightstand and a chest of drawers. A wide door

Room 114 at Many Glacier Hotel

Bathroom in room 114 at Many Glacier Hotel

leads out to a shared balcony, which offers a good view of the lake, and has plenty of room for a wheelchair or scooter.

The bathroom has a full five-foot turning radius and is equipped with a roll-in shower with grab bars, a hand-held showerhead and a fold-down shower bench. Other access features include toilet grab bars on the back and right walls (as seated), and a roll-under sink with a lowered mirror. This room is much larger than room 114, so it's a better choice for folks with power wheelchairs or scooters.

Room 102 at Many Glacier Hotel

Bathroom in room 102 at Many Glacier Hotel

There's good access to all of the public areas on the lobby and ground levels of this property, including the Ptarmigan Dining Room and the Swiss Lounge; and there's an elevator located near the Ptarmigan Dining Room. Accessible family restrooms are located on both levels; and there is also barrier-free access to the Lucerne Room on the lobby level, where ranger programs are often held.

The Many Glacier Hotel is open from mid-June to mid-September.

Swiftcurrent Motor Inn

Many Glacier Valley
Glacier National Park, MT 59434
(855) 733-4522
www.glaciernationalparklodges.com

Located at the end of the park road, just a mile east of Many Glacier Lodge, the Swiftcurrent Motor Inn features standard motel rooms and rustic cabins dotted throughout the forested property.

Accessible parking is located near the main building, with ramp access up to the front porch, and level access through a wide door to the main lobby. There are several doors into the main building, but the one that goes through Nell's Restaurant, on the far left of the building, offers the best wheelchair access. There's wheelchair access to all of the public facilities in the main lodge building, including a set of restrooms with accessible stalls and roll-under sinks, located near the registration desk.

The rooms and cabins are located a short drive from the main lodge building. Four accessible motel rooms are located in the Motel 3 building,

Main Building at Swiftcurrent Motor Inn

which features accessible parking and level access over to the building.

Room 41 is features good pathway access and is furnished with a 27-inch high double bed with wheelchair access on the left (as you face it), a bedside table

Motel building 3 at Swiftcurrent Motor Inn

Room 41 at Swiftcurrent Motor Inn

and a chest of drawers. The bathroom has a roll-in shower with a slight one-inch lip, with grab bars, a hand-held showerhead and a fold-down shower seat. The toilet grab bars are located on the back and right walls (as seated), and the bathroom also includes a roll-under sink with a lowered mirror.

Room 42 and room 29 have the same access features as room 41. Room 40 is a mirror image of room 41, with the toilet grab bars on the back and left walls (as seated).

Bathroom in room 41 at Swiftcurrent Motor Inn

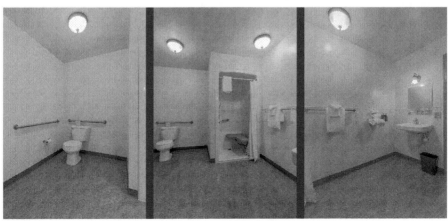

Cabin I-1 at Swiftcurrent Motor Inn

Cabin I-1 is located next to the public shower and laundry facilities, and includes accessible parking next to the unit on a cement pad. Access features include wide doorways, good pathway access and a laminate floor for easy rolling. The unit is furnished with two 27-inch high

Bedroom in cabin I-1 at Swiftcurrent Motor Inn

Bathroom in cabin I-1 at Swiftcurrent Motor Inn

double beds, with wheelchair access in the middle and right side (as you face them), a night table, and a small table with two chairs. A large laundry-type sink is also located in the main room. Add in a nostalgic screen door and a small accessible front porch, and you feel like you're in grandma's cabin in the woods.

The bathroom includes a full five-foot turning radius and is equipped with a roll-in shower with grab bars, a hand-held showerhead and a fold-down shower bench. The toilet grab bars are located on the back and right walls (as seated), and there's also a roll-under sink with an angled mirror in the bathroom.

It's a pleasant property with affordable rooms, and a decidedly mountain atmosphere. There are no televisions or internet access here, but that only adds to the ambiance. If, on the other hand, you need to make an emergency call, lowered pay phones are located near the main building.

The Swiftcurrent Motor Inn is open from mid-June to mid-September.

Access Overview

One of the most accessible ways to see the park is to take a drive on Going-to-the-Sun Road, which runs from West Glacier on the west to St. Mary on the east. There are lots of accessible overlooks and some great windshield views along the way. Logan Pass, which is located midway along the route, is worth a stop too, as there's a scenic quarter-mile wheelchair-accessible trail behind the visitor center. Logan Pass is the highest point in the park navigable by vehicle, with an elevation of 6,646 feet. Elevations in the majority of the other touristed areas of the park range from 3,000 to 4,500 feet.

There's also a free accessible shuttle from Apgar Visitor Center and St. Mary Visitor Center to Logan Pass during the summer months. Both routes offer stops at the major viewpoints along Going-to-the-Sun Road; however express service is also available. All shuttle buses are either ramp or lift-equipped and have tie-downs.

There are several accessible trails on the west side of the park, including the Apgar Bike Path, which runs .4 mile from the visitor center to Apgar Village, and then continues another 2.6 miles through the woods to West Glacier. There's also a short quarter-mile spur that connects Apgar Campground to the Apgar Visitor Center. This undulating asphalt trail is wide and kept in good repair.

Apgar Loop Trail

The Apgar Loop begins to the left of the backcountry office on Apgar Loop Road, and follows the Apgar Bike Path for about .1 mile. From there, it circles right through the woods to the Apgar Bridge over McDonald Creek, and then returns through another stretch of woods to Eddie's Restaurant on Apgar Loop Road. From there it's just a short level roll down the sidewalk to the backcountry office. This asphalt trail is wide and level, and even though it's close to the village, it feels like you are miles away in the woods. It's a good option for folks who cant manage the longer Apgar Bike Path.

Over at Lake McDonald, a short paved path begins on the right of Lake McDonald Lodge and winds through the forest past the cabins along the lakeshore. It ends near cabin 12, and although it's only .15-mile long, it makes a pleasant stroll.

One of the most accessible trails in the park — The Trail of the Cedars — is located along Going-to-the-Sun Road, next to the Avalanche Campground. It offers an .8-mile barrier-free trek through a cedar and hemlock forest, alongside a peaceful mountain stream. You can begin the trail next to the Avalanche Creek bridge, where an accessible boardwalk travels .1 mile through the forest, before it transitions to a hard-packed dirt and asphalt trail. From there the trail meanders alongside the creek for another .4 miles, before it crosses an accessible footbridge and reverts back to a boardwalk.

Trail of the Cedars in Glacier National Park

The footbridge provides a splendid view of the cascading waters in lower Avalanche Gorge, and offers a quiet place to reflect and take a break.

Over on the east side of the park, a quarter-mile section of the Swiftcurrent Lake Trail is now accessible, thanks to some recent upgrades. The trailhead is located in the Grinnell Glacier Trailhead parking area, just a short walk from the accessible restrooms. The wide hard-packed dirt trail winds through a lodgepole pine forest and over a small creek, before four steps block further access. There are benches along the trail, and even one near the creek. It makes a nice out-and-back half-mile hike; and the bench near the creek is a great spot to stop for a picnic.

Located about a mile west of the Two Medicine Entrance, the Running Eagle Falls Trail is also a good choice for wheelers and slow walkers. The hard-packed dirt trail leads a quarter-mile through the forest to a vantage point on the beach. From there you can get a nice view of Running Eagle Falls. On the return trip, take a right on the nature trail for a pleasant — and quiet — walk alongside the river. This .3-mile hard-packed dirt trail comes out on the far end of the parking lot, and it makes a nice alternative to the crowded main trail.

Don't Miss This

A small but accessible stop on Highway 2, midway between West Glacier and Two Medicine, may yield a prime wildlife viewing opportunity. Goat Lick Overlook is well marked from the west, but there is no signage on the east, so look for the turnout on the left, just past mile marker 183. There's accessible parking next to a paved 200-foot level path out to the overlook, where – if you're lucky – you'll be able to spot mountain goats on the "lick" to the right. If not, don't be disappointed, as there's also a good view of the middle fork of the Flathead River on the left.

Insider Tip

Although the historic Red Buses of Glacier National Park are not wheelchair-accessible, the Xanterra Travel Collection added two wheelchair-accessible vehicles to their fleet when they took over as concessionaire in 2014. The lift-equipped vehicles have two-wheelchair spaces with tie-downs, and can accommodate a total of 14 passengers. The buses have roll-up plastic flaps on the windows, so passengers get the same open-air experience that's available on the historic buses. An oxygen tank holder and a power outlet are also located in the first row of seats. And passengers get a full view of everything around them, thanks to an on-board camera and monitors. The camera, which can be controlled by a passenger, can rotate a full 360 degrees, and even move in for close-ups. It's great for spotting wildlife.

It should be noted that these accessible vehicles are not solely for wheelchair-users. Slow walkers, people who use canes, or anyone who feels they can't manage the two narrow 18-inch high steps on the historic vehicles, and then slide over on a bench seat, are welcome to book a tour in an accessible vehicle. As an added bonus, the vehicles are also air conditioned. Even better, your party will have the entire bus to themselves. It's like having a private tour — and the guides are excellent.

The accessible tours generally follow the same itinerary as the standard tours; however they tend to spend more time at the accessible stops, such as the Trail of the Cedars and Logan Pass. Advance reservations are required, and since these tours are extremely popular, it's best to book as early as possible.

Adapted Red Bus in Glacier National Park

Resources

Glacier National Park
(406) 888-7800
www.nps.gov/glac
www.facebook.com/GlacierNPS
twitter.com/GlacierNPS

Road Conditions
(406) 888-7800

Red Bus Tours
(855) 733-4522
www.glaciernationalparklodges.com

Xanterra Travel Collection (NPS Concessionaire)
(855) 733-4522
www.glaciernationalparklodges.com
twitter.com/GlacierLodges
Village Inn at Apgar
Lake McDonald Lodge
Rising Sun Motor Inn
Many Glacier Hotel
Swiftcurrent Motor Inn

Pursuit
(844) 868-7474 (NPS Concessionaire)
www.glacierparkcollection.com
Motel Lake McDonald

Barrier-Free Travels; Glacier, Yellowstone and Grand Teton National Parks for Wheelers and Slow Walkers
www.barrierfreeyellowstone.com

Ohio

Station Road Bridge in Cuyahoga Valley National Park

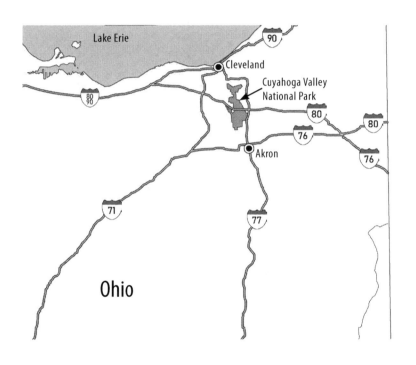

Cuyahoga Valley National Park

This Northeastern Ohio national park takes its name from the Iroquois word for crooked river — Cuyahoga. And indeed the Cuyahoga River literally snakes through the park, past 33,000 acres of forested hills, bordered by what was once the Ohio & Erie Canal Towpath. Today, the towpath is still intact, but the mule traffic has been replaced by cyclists and hikers. And because of the level grade of the towpath, it's an excellent trail for wheelchair-users and slow walkers.

Located between Cleveland and Akron, the park can be accessed by car, bicycle or on the railway. Paved roads bisect the park and parallel the towpath, with plenty of spots to stop and smell the flowers along the way. Cuyahoga Valley National Park is also the only national park that has a rail line that runs through it, with three main boarding stations in the park. No matter your mode of transportation, you'll be treated to scenic beauty and a wide variety of wildlife in Ohio's only national park.

There are no official entrance stations to the park, so the best way to access it is to travel along the two main park roads — Canal Road and Riverview Road — from Cleveland or Akron. Canal Road connects to Riverview Road near the Brecksville Station via Chaffee Road and Highway 82, and this scenic route offers uninterrupted access to both sections of the park.

From Cleveland, take Interstate 77 south to Brecksville Road in Independence. Go south on Brecksville Road, turn east on Rockside Road, and then head south on Canal Road to enter the park near Rockside Station. It's about a 10-mile drive.

From Akron, go north on Merriman Road near Sand Run Metro Park. Merriman Road turns into Riverview Road, and enters the park near Botzum, about four miles up the road.

Cuyahoga Valley National Park is open year-round; however a small area — from Fitzwater to the Route 82 bridge — is usually closed to pedestrian traffic during the bald eagle nesting season. This closure generally runs from February to August.

There are two lodges in Cuyahoga Valley National Park, one of which is wheelchair-accessible.

Admission

There is no entrance fee to Cuyahoga Valley National Park.

Spend the Night

Stanford House

6093 Stanford Road
Peninsula, OH
(330) 657-2909 ext. 130
www.conservancyforcvnp.org/experience/plan-your-visit/retreats-lodging

Located near the Boston Mills Visitor Center, this historic house is a favorite venue for group events; however many visitors don't realize that it's also open to individual visitors if it's not booked by a group. It's a beautiful old house, and a very secluded and peaceful place to spend the night in Cuyahoga Valley National Park.

There's accessible parking in front of the office, which is located next to the historic two-story home, with a barrier-free pathway over to the accessible walkway up to the front porch. The grand old home features wide doorways, wood floors, good pathway access and wheelchair access on

The Stanford House in Cuyahoga Valley National Park

the first floor. The home is decorated with vintage wallpaper, grand wood moldings and historic chandeliers; while several comfortable rocking chairs line the accessible front porch.

The living room is furnished with a sofa, two love seats, a settee and a few chairs; and there's still plenty of room to maneuver a wheelchair or scooter around the period pieces and reproductions. The dining room is massive and it includes two long wooden tables which each can seat 16 people. There's a small hutch which is filled with cups, plates, glasses and dishes; and the adjacent commercial kitchen is equipped with a refrigerator, freezer, microwave, and just about every small appliance and utensil you can imagine.

The accessible guestroom — number 9 — is located just around the corner. It's furnished with two 19-inch high twin beds with wheelchair access on both sides, as well as a trundle daybed that has a 21-inch high mattress and an eleven-inch high mattress. Truly wheelchair-users have their choice of bed heights in this home. Top it off with a lowered bedroom mirror and you have a nice accessible room.

The adjacent bathroom features a full five-foot turning radius and is equipped with a 36-inch square transfer shower, with a fold-down shower bench, grab bars and a hand-held-showerhead. There's ample floor space in front of the shower to transfer to the shower bench, and level access to roll-in to the unit for folks that bring their own shower chairs. Other bathroom access features

Living room in the Stanford House

Dining room in the Stanford House

include a roll-under sink, and a toilet with a grab bar on the left side (as seated).

The upstairs bedrooms, which feature two shared bathrooms are set up as a dormitory, and are only accessible by stairs.

Room 9 in the Stanford House (view 1)

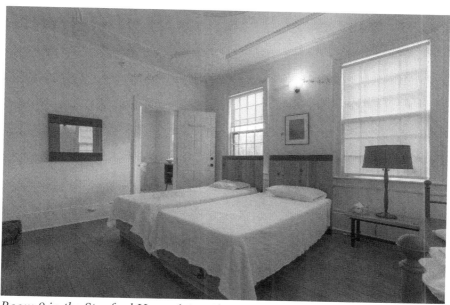

Room 9 in the Stanford House (view 2)

Outside there's level access to a picnic table on the lawn, and the nearby fire circle. Truly the folks at the Conservatory for Cuyahoga Valley National Park thought of everything at Stanford House, including insect repellent, lawn chairs and two charcoal grills. Additionally, if they know a wheelchair-user will be

Bathroom adjacent to room 9 in the Stanford House

staying at the house, the staff is quite good about making sure necessary items — like the first-aid kit — are placed on the lower shelves. As an added bonus, the house also has Wi-Fi, which is kind of spotty throughout the rest of the park.

Stanford House can accommodate groups of up to 30 people, and it's a good choice for an accessible event. Individual accessible bookings — which include a private room and bathroom, with shared access to the first-floor common rooms — are available two weeks in advance. And if there aren't any other individual bookings, you'll have the home to yourself.

Stanford House is open year-round.

Access Overview

The best way to explore the park is to drive along Canal Road and Riverview Road, and stop at some of the accessible trails and sights along the way. The highest elevation in the park is 1,164 feet at Brush Road, and the lowest elevation is 590 feet at the Cuyahoga River, so most folks won't experience any altitude-related issues.

The Canal Exploration Center, which is located on the north end of the park, is a good place to begin your visit. There's accessible parking with paved access to the accessible front entrance of this former 1800s tavern, which now houses a store and an information center. And since the paved towpath runs right in front of the building, you can take a short hike in either direction.

Brecksville Nature Center, which is located a short drive south, is also worth a stop. Accessible parking is located next to an accessible picnic table, so pack along a lunch and enjoy a midday break. From there it's a .15-mile walk on an accessible trail to the nature center. Accessible restrooms are located next door, and there's level access to the nature center, which features a number of interpretive exhibits. The building also boasts floor-to-ceiling windows that overlook the garden bird feeders. It's an excellent place to sit back and enjoy some of the 200-plus different avian visitors that have been spotted in the park.

Station Road Bridge, which is located near the Brecksville Depot, is just a short drive away, near the intersection of Chippewa Creek Drive and Riverview Road. There's accessible parking near the station, and it's just a 250-foot level walk out this metal truss bridge which is listed on the National Register of Historic Places. Bring along binoculars, and you may get a glimpse of more avian life near the Pinery Narrows — the narrowest

Brandywine Falls in Cuyahoga Valley National Park

part of the Cuyahoga River. There's also a good view of the Brecksville-Northfield High Level Bridge on Ohio Route 82, which was built in 1931. And if you're lucky, the Cuyahoga Valley Scenic Railroad excursion train might even pull into the Brecksville Station.

Continue south on Riverview Road, turn east on Vaughn Road, then head South on Brandywine Road to get to Brandywine Falls, one of the park's most popular attractions. There's accessible parking near the accessible restrooms, with level access to a 150-foot paved trail, that transitions to an accessible boardwalk through the forest. An accessible overlook at the end of the boardwalk offers a magnificent view of the 65-foot high falls as it cascades down over a shale wall into Brandywine Creek. Unfortunately there are steps down to the lower overlook, but you can still get a good view from the top.

Back on Riverview Road, continue south, then turn west on Everett Road for a look at the Everett Covered Bridge. There's accessible parking next to a level paved trail that leads out to this historic Smith Truss structure. It's just a .15-mile walk, and there's also level access to the bridge, so you can walk or roll across it. Additionally, there's a short 70-foot hard-packed dirt path over to a level area which offers an excellent bridge view. And if you'd like to linger on and enjoy it all, there are also a few benches there.

Finally, don't miss the heronry, just north of Botzum, near the southern park boundary. From Riverview Road, go east on Bath Road, to a small

Everett Covered Bridge in Cuyahoga Valley National Park

wayside area on the left. There's no striped parking, but there's room enough to parallel park in the paved area near the heronry. You can catch a view of the herons nesting in the treetops across the street from from the viewing area, which is about 15 feet away. Plan ahead though, as the herons are only in residence from February until late July.

Don't Miss This

If you only have time to do one thing in Cuyahoga Valley National Park, then make sure and take the 2.5-hour scenic excursion on the Cuyahoga Valley Scenic Railroad. It's a great way to get a good overview of the park, and access aboard is top-drawer with a purpose-built accessible car.

There's accessible parking next to the Rockside Station in Independence, level access over to the ticket counter, and an accessible vault toilet nearby. And if you can't walk far, a loaner wheelchair is available for boarding. There's lift access to the accessible car, which came from the Central of Georgia Railroad and dates back to the 1940s. After a $250,000 renovation, the car now has 60 seats, all of which can be flipped up to accommodate wheelchair-users. Top it off with a large accessible restroom and you have a very inclusive and accessible car.

The 2.5-hour national park excursion travels south from the Rockside

Boarding the Cuyahoga Valley Scenic Railroad

Station, along the scenic Cuyahoga River, and presents numerous opportunities for wildlife viewing. Volunteers are on board to point out sights along the way, but keep your eyes peeled for the eagle nest — and the resident eagles — just north of Brecksville. The train continues south past the Boston Store Visitor Center and Peninsula Depot, and finally winds its way down to the Akron Northside Station. After that, it turns around and heads back to the Rockside Station. It's an excellent way to get a good overview of the park, and to make note of places you may want to return to for a longer visit. And you just can't beat the scenery.

Insider Tip

For some good wildlife viewing, head down to the Beaver Boardwalk. Park in the Ira Trailhead Parking, just south of Howe Meadow on Riverview Road, and follow the asphalt trail over to the towpath. From there, it's a quarter-mile walk on the level trail, out to the .20-mile boardwalk over Beaver Marsh. The access is excellent, and it's a pleasant one-mile round trip ramble through the woods. Plan a visit near dusk or dawn for optimal beaver viewing. The marsh is also alive with waterfowl during the migration in March and November.

Beaver Boardwalk in Cuyahoga Valley National Park

Resources

Cuyahoga Valley National Park
(330) 657-2752
www.nps.gov/cuva
www.facebook.com/CuyahogaValleyNationalPark
twitter.com/CVNPNPS

Conservancy for Cuyahoga Valley National Park (NPS Concessionaire)
(330) 657-2909 ext. 130
www.conservancyforcvnp.org/experience/plan-your-visit/retreats-lodging
www.facebook.com/ConservancyCVNP
twitter.com/forcvnp
Stanford House

Cuyahoga Valley Scenic Railroad
(800) 468-4070
www.cvsr.com

Oregon

Phantom Ship Island in Crater Lake National Park

Crater Lake National Park

L ocated at 7,100 feet along Southern Oregon's Cascade Crest, Crater Lake was created over 7,700 years ago after a massive eruption of Mount Mazama. The resulting caldera filled with melted snow and rainwater, and subsequently the 1943-foot-deep lake took on a deep blue — and somewhat ethereal — hue. And although the lakeshore itself is not wheelchair-accessible, slow walkers and wheelchair-users can get an equally enthralling view from Rim Drive which circles the lake, or from historic — but accessible — Crater Lake Ledge.

There are two entrances to Crater Lake National Park.

The west entrance is located on Highway 62, about 1.5 hours northeast of Medford, or an hour north of Klamath Falls.

The north entrance, which is closed to vehicles in the winter, is located about four hours south of Portland, on Highway 138.

Although the park is open year-round, most of the concessions and facilities are closed during the winter. The North Entrance and Rim Drive can close for the season to vehicular traffic as early as October. After that Rim Drive becomes a trail for snowshoers and skiers. The North Entrance reopens between mid-May and late June; and Rim Drive opens between mid-June and late July. The opening and closing dates depend on the amount of snow.

The West Entrance is open year-round, as is the seven-mile road from Highway 62 to Rim Village; however the last three miles of that road may temporarily close during heavy snows. And although Park Headquarters and the visitor center are open year-round, food and lodging concessions are closed in the winter. The best time to visit the park is usually from July to September.

Crater Lake National Park has one lodge.

Admission

$25 – seven-day pass (May 22 – October 31)
$15 – seven day pass (November 1 – May 21)
$50 – yearly pass

Spend the Night

Crater Lake Lodge

565 Rim Drive
Crater Lake National Park, OR 97604
(866) 292-6720
www.craterlakelodges.com

Historic Crater Lake Lodge dates back to 1915, when this lakeside beauty welcomed travelers who journeyed for days over unpaved trails and roads to visit the caldera lake. Over the years more creature comforts were added, but sadly the structure itself was in danger of failing. Finally in 1991 an ambitious $15 million renovation project began. Over the next four years the building was gutted and a new structural support system and modern hotel amenities were added. Today this National Register property is once again the grand old lady of the lake, only now she sports some upgraded access features.

Although steps grace the front entrance of the property, there's also ramp access on the left side. Accessible parking is located around the corner near the side door, which is just steps from the accessible rooms. Additionally there's a drop-off area in front, for folks who can't manage distances.

Historic Crater Lake Lodge

Room 107 at historic Crater Lake Lodge

Inside, there's plenty of room to maneuver a wheelchair around the cavernous lobby, which is dominated by a massive stone fireplace. There's barrier-free access to the front desk as well as the first-floor rooms.

Bathroom in room 107 at historic Crater Lake Lodge

Crater Lake Lodge has six accessible rooms, all of which are equipped with tub/shower combinations.

Room 107 is just down the hall from the lobby. This accessible room features wide doorways, a lowered peephole, and plenty of room to maneuver a wheelchair or scooter inside. It's furnished with a 26-inch high queen-sized bed with wheelchair access on both sides, a desk with a chair, and a side chair.

The bathroom is equipped with a tub/shower combination with grab bars, a hand-held showerhead and a fold-down tub bench. The toilet grab bars are located on the back and right walls (as seated), and the bathroom also has a roll-under sink. And like the bedroom, the bathroom is very spacious, with plenty of room for a wheelchair or scooter.

Additionally, in keeping with the ambience of days gone by, the guest room is pleasantly devoid of a phone and a television — as are the remaining 70 guest rooms.

There is also good access to the public areas of the lodge, including the great hall, the terrace and the dining room. Even if you don't stay at Crater Lake Lodge, stop in and enjoy a drink or a snack on the terrace, as it offers one of the best views of Crater Lake. And if it's a little chilly outside, try and snag a window table in the adjacent restaurant. The property exudes a definite 1920s charm, yet it has all the creature comforts of a modern day property.

Crater Lake Lodge is open from mid-May to mid-October.

Access Overview

The most accessible way to enjoy Crater Lake is to take the 31-mile Rim Drive that circles the caldera. For the best windshield views take the drive in a counterclockwise direction starting on West Rim Drive. There are a number of overlooks and pullouts along the drive, but the windshield views are also spectacular. The elevation along the rim ranges from 7,000 to 8,000 feet, so take it slow until you are acclimated.

The most accessible of the named overlooks is Watchman Overlook, which offers an excellent view of Wizard Island. There's accessible parking near the accessible vault toilet, with curb-cut access to a sidewalk over to the lower overlook. The upper overlook is only accessible by stairs or a steep path, but don't fret if you can't make it to the top, as you'll catch some of the best

Cloudcap Overlook at Crater Lake National Park

views from the road. Cloudcap Overlook and Phantom Ship Overlook also offer some great windshield views of the lake. And don't miss Vidae Falls on the last section of East Rim Drive, as this 100-foot waterfall can be easily seen from the pullout.

Pack along a picnic lunch and stop at one of the accessible picnic areas along Rim Drive. White Bark Pine Picnic Area is located on East Rim Drive and features an accessible vault toilet and an accessible picnic table on a level dirt area. There's also an accessible picnic area near the Crater Peak Trail just off East Rim Drive. There's accessible parking near the accessible vault toilet and level access over to the accessible picnic table.

If you'd like to leave the driving to someone else, Crater Lake Trolley offers an accessible tour which travels along Rim Drive and stops at five to seven viewpoints. This two-hour ranger-led tour departs from Rim Village, and the lift-equipped trolley has space for two manual wheelchairs. It should be noted that power wheelchairs or scooters cannot be accommodated, and manual wheelchairs must be no wider than 28-inches and have a combined weight limit of 400 pounds. Reservations can be made in person or by phone.

The Godfrey Glen Trail, which is the most accessible trail in the park, is also a good choice for folks with power wheelchairs or scooters. It's located near the south park entrance on Munson Valley Road. This hard-packed dirt trail passes through an old growth hemlock and fir forest; and although there are some ruts and roots along the way, most are easy to dodge. The

179

biggest obstacle along this 1.1-mile loop is the steep grade on a few sections. Best bet it to travel in a clockwise direction, and double back when it gets too steep. Even if you can't complete the whole trail, you'll still get some nice canyon views along the way. This trail received some serious weather-related damage in 2019, and at press time it was still closed for repairs. Check the park website for closure updates.

Insider Tip

Although the Rim Drive is a must-do on any Crater Lake visit, save some time to hop off-the-beaten-path to explore two accessible trails off of Pinnacles Road. Located on the south side of the lake, this seven-mile road begins near Phantom Ship Overlook, and runs out to Pinnacles Overlook, near the southeastern border of the park. The road and the overlook are named for the spire-like pumice formations that dot this river valley. Accessible parking is located next to the Pinnacles Trail, which offers a closer look at these unusual formations, that were created when hot volcanic gases shot up through the ash.

The Pinnacles Trail passes by several overlooks that offer good views of the formations. The hard-packed dirt trail is covered in crushed rock, and although it's not entirely level, the undulations are doable for most

Pinnacles Trail at Crater Lake National Park

Plaikni Falls Trail at Crater Lake National Park

wheelchair-users. Even if you can't manage the whole half-mile hike to the park boundary, at least take the level 250-foot walk out to the first overlook. You won't be disappointed.

The Plaikni Falls Trail, which is located near the beginning of Pinnacles Road is also worth a stop. Accessible parking is located near this trail which winds through an old growth forest to the base of the falls. That said, the last quarter-mile is extremely steep, and probably not doable for most wheelchair-users and slow walkers. On the other hand, the stroll through the forest is fairly level, and there are numerous wheelchair turn-outs and benches located along the way.

And although Pinnacles Road makes a nice outing, be forewarned that there are no accessible toilets at either trailhead. Best bet is to plan ahead and make a rest stop at White Bark Pine Picnic Area or the Crater Peak Trail Picnic Area before hitting the trails.

Don't Miss This

Take some time to enjoy the rim view on foot on the accessible section of the Rim Village Promenade, which runs alongside the rim from the Rim Village Café and Gift Shop to the back terrace of Crater Lake Lodge.

Accessible parking is located near the gift shop, with paved access to the trail behind the gift shop. When you get to the rim, make a right and continue along .3-miles until you hit the lodge.

Interpretive plaques are located along the way, and it's the perfect spot for a selfie or two, as the views are grand. The trail is mostly paved, and undulating, with a slight change in elevation just past Kiser Studio. Still, most manual wheelchair-users can manage the grade with a little assistance. Alternatively, there's ramp access down to the trail from the back terrace at Crater Lake Lodge. Either way, the views at both ends of the trail are equally impressive. The trail continues on past Crater Lake Lodge, but it loses its access due to the steep grade.

Rim Village Promenade at Crater Lake National Park

Resources

Crater Lake National Park
(541) 594-3000
www.nps.gov/crla
www.facebook.com/Crater-Lake-National-Park-137127376328525
twitter.com/CraterLakeNPS

Aramark (NPS Concessionaire)
(866) 292-6720
www.travelcraterlake.com
www.facebook.com/TravelCraterLake
Crater Lake Lodge

Crater Lake Trolley
(541) 882-1896
www.craterlaketrolley.net

Back terrace at Crater Lake Lodge

South Dakota

Doors Trail in Badlands National Park

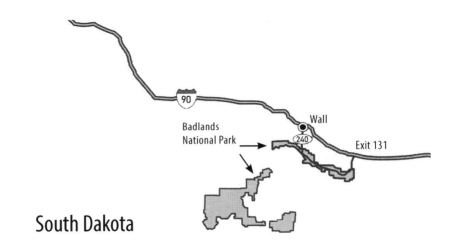

90

Wall

Badlands
National Park

240

Exit 131

South Dakota

The Window Trail is located on the south side of the parking lot. The level boardwalk leads out to a natural window the frames eerie hoodoo-like formations off in the distance. It's a pleasant quarter-mile out-and-back stroll.

The Door Trail is located at the other end of the parking lot, near the much needed shade structure. The level boardwalk snakes between a break in the Badlands Wall — called The Door — and opens up to a sweeping sandstone canyon view at the end. It's a .75-mile round trip hike, and if you need a break, there are a few benches along the way.

The Fossil Exhibit Trail, which is located near White River Valley Overlook, is also worth a stop. Accessible parking and an accessible vault toilet are located near the trailhead. This quarter-mile boardwalk features low bumpers for unobstructed views, and includes interpretive panels that describe the extinct creatures that once roamed the area. Examples of fossils are also located along this nicely accessible loop trail.

Each trail offers a different look at the varied landscape, but don't forget the sunscreen, as shade is in short supply in this neck of the woods. Summer temperatures can also get pretty severe, so make sure and carry an ample supply of water too.

End of the Window Trail in Badlands National Park

Don't Miss This

Most wheelchair-users and slow walkers drive right past the Cliff Shelf Nature Trail because it's not accessible. Granted, the bulk of this boardwalk trail is steep, with a number of steps along the way; however it's still worth a stop for the initial views. Accessible parking is located near a ramp to the viewpoint, where you'll be treated to a sweeping view of the White River Valley. A short section of the boardwalk is accessible, so keep going until you hit the steps. It's also one of the few areas of the park that has some vegetation.

Insider Tip

Although Cedar Pass Lodge has a full-service restaurant, pack along a picnic lunch to enjoy at one of the most scenic viewpoints in the park — Bigfoot Pass Overlook. Located about eight miles north of Cedar Pass Lodge, this small picnic area features accessible parking, with barrier-free access over to a shaded table. And you just can't beat the panoramic badlands view. It does get pretty windy in this area though, so be sure to hang on to your napkin.

Cliff Shelf Nature Trail in Badlands National Park

Resources

Badlands National Park
(605) 433-5361
www.nps.gov/badl
www.facebook.com/BadlandsNPS
twitter.com/BadlandsNPS

Road Conditions
(605) 433-5361

Forever Resorts (NPS Concessionaire)
(877) 386-4383
www.cedarpasslodge.com
Cedar Pass Lodge

Fossil Exhibit Trail in Badlands National Park

Texas

Panther Path at Big Bend National Park

Big Bend National Park

Named for the giant bend in the Rio Grande that carves out the southern border of the park, Big Bend National Park is located in Southwestern Texas, more than 100 miles from the nearest freeway, hospital or shopping mall. Our neighbors to the south call it El Despoblado — the uninhabited land — an appropriate nickname for the 800,000-acre expanse. And although this remote park features a chunk of weather-beaten desert, and some high backcountry peaks, there are still plenty of accessible overlooks, trails and attractions for wheelchair-users and slow walkers to enjoy.

Big Bend National Park has two entrances.

The Persimmon Gap Entrance is located on the north side of the park, about 40 miles south of Marathon.

The Study Butte Entrance can be found on the west side, approximately 80 miles south of Alpine.

There is also a port of entry near Boquillas Mexico; however the border crossing involves a short trip across the Rio Grande on an inaccessible rowboat.

Big Bend National Park is open year-round; however the port of entry has limited days and hours of operation.

There is one lodge in Big Bend National Park.

Admission

$30 – seven-day pass

$55 – yearly pass

Spend the Night

Chisos Mountains Lodge

1 Basin Rural Station
Big Bend National Park, TX 79834
(432) 477-2291
www.chisosmountainslodge.com

Located in the Chisos Basin, this comfortable property is located well away from the maddening city crowds, yet boasts all the creature comforts of home. There's accessible parking in front of the office, with level access to the main lobby through automatic doors. Inside there's plenty of room to maneuver a wheelchair over to the front desk and the gift shop. The accessible rooms are located a short drive away in the newer Casa Grande section of the property.

Accessible parking is located in front of room D2 — an accessible ground floor room — with sidewalk access over to the front door. Some manual wheelchair-users may require a bit of assistance up the sidewalk, as there is one section that has an uphill grade. Access features in room D2 include wide doorways, a lowered peephole, lever handles, good pathway access and tile floors for easy rolling.

Room D2 at Chisos Mountains Lodge in Big Bend National Park (view 1)

Room D2 at Chisos Mountains Lodge in Big Bend National Park (view 2)

The room is furnished with a 25-inch high open-frame double bed with wheelchair access on the left side '(as you face the bed). That said, there's plenty of room to move the bed if you require wheelchair access on the opposite side. Other furnishings include a night stand, two easy chairs, a

Bathroom in room D2 at Chisos Mountains Lodge in Big Bend National Park

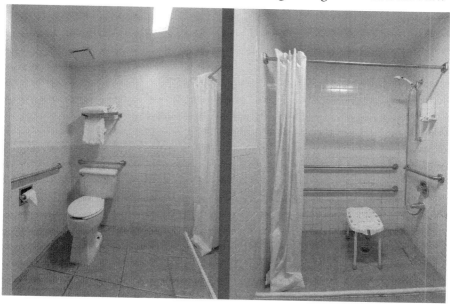

dresser, a refrigerator and a microwave. Best of all, the room also has level access out to the shared back patio, which is furnished with two chairs and a table. It's the perfect place to enjoy one of Big Bend's most impressive features — the dark night sky.

There's barrier-free access to the bathroom which features a roll-in shower with grab bars and a hand-held showerhead. The toilet grab bars are located on the back and right walls (as seated), and a portable shower bench is available upon request. A roll-under sink is located in the adjacent sleeping area, to free up more room space in the bathroom.

It's important to note that if you use any type of wheelchair or scooter, you'll need to book an accessible room at Chisos Mountains Lodge. This applies even if you don't need an adapted bathroom, because the accessible rooms are the only guest rooms with wide doorways.

Room D2 is located just across the parking lot from the visitor center and the Basin Store. There's ramp access up to the store with accessible parking in front, and barrier-free access over to the visitor center and accessible public restrooms.

The Chisos Mountains Lodge Restaurant is located just a short walk away from the Casa Grande section of the property; however since it's on an uphill grade it's best to drive. There's barrier-free access through the lobby and gift shop to the restaurant. The menu features a good variety of Tex-Mex dishes, as well as traditional American favorites. Don't miss the deck – it's a great place to enjoy a glass of wine and take in what can only be described as one of the best views in Texas.

Chisos Mountains Lodge is open year-round.

Access Overview

Although there's certainly a good portion of backcountry in Big Bend National Park, there are a number of accessible sites and facilities in the more developed areas of the park. The elevation ranges from 1,800 feet along the Rio Grande, to 7,832 feet on top of Emory Peak, with Panther Visitor Center clocking in at a very reasonable 3,750 feet. Summer temperatures on the desert floor often top 100 degrees, so get an early start if you visit during that time of year.

Although there's no shortage of great windshield views in the park, there are also a few accessible trails. Panther Path, which is located next to the

Panther Visitor Center offers a short — but accessible — introduction to some of the plants found in the park. Accessible parking is located near the visitor center, with level access over to this short 100-yard sidewalk lined with interpretive plaques that identify desert plants. Accessible restrooms are also located at the visitor center, which makes a good stop to get a brief orientation of the park.

A portion of the Rio Grande Village Nature Trail is also a good choice for wheelchair-users and slow walkers. It's located in the southeast area of the park, near Boquillas Canyon. The trailhead is actually located in the campground at Rio Grande Village, across from campsite 18. Parking is limited near the trailhead, with just a few pullouts along the road. The best choice for accessible parking is in front of the restroom, across from campsite 12. From there, follow the campground road around towards campsite 18 to access the trail.

The trail begins with a short dirt path to the quarter-mile boardwalk over the pond. Some folks may need a bit of assistance over the dirt trail, as it's a bit bumpy, but the floating boardwalk offers excellent access, and it's a great spot to enjoy the sunrise or sunset. It's also an excellent birding location.

The Fossil Bone Exhibit, which is located eight miles north of Panther Junction, is also worth a stop. The newest addition to the park, this site features accessible parking with barrier-free access to the shaded

Rio Grande Village Nature Trail in Big Bend National Park

Fosil Bone Exhibit in Big Bend National Park

interpretive exhibits about creatures that roamed the area some 63 to 72 million years ago. The result of a $1.4 million project, the exhibit offers plenty of room for wheelchair-users and slow walkers to maneuver around the interpretive panels, and roll right up to life-size skull replicas of some former residents. There's also an accessible vault toilet and a shaded picnic area with accessible tables at this site.

By far the highlight of any Big Bend visit is what most folks describe as "the" drive in the park — the Ross Maxwell Scenic Drive. This 30-mile route leads past the Castolon Historic District and Santa Elena Canyon, and passes through some historic and geologic treasures along the way. The drive takes about 45 minutes one-way, but be sure to allow extra time to stop and admire the scenery.

The drive begins just off the main park road, with a south turn at Castolon - Santa Elena Junction. There are a number of scenic overlooks along the way, including the Homer Wilson Ranch Overlook and Mule Ears Viewpoint — both of which have accessible parking with barrier-free access out to the viewpoints. The former features views of the old ranch house and surrounding land, while the latter offers the best vantage point for a glance at the iconic Mule Ears rock formation.

Located between those two overlooks, Goat Mountain Viewpoint features accessible parking with ramp access out to the overlook. Be sure and watch for road signs for this viewpoint, as it's not on the park map. Sotol Vista — which is named for the native plant that thrives there — also has accessible parking, an accessible pit toilet, and barrier-free access to the overlook which offers a panoramic southern view.

Last but not least, don't miss the Santa Elena Overlook at the end of the road. From the overlook you can gaze down at the limestone canyon created by the Rio Grande, and look across into neighboring Mexico. Although there's no curb-cut access from the parking area to the overlook, you can wheel down to where the curb ends and roll out to the overlook. Even though the ground is a bit bumpy in places, it's still doable for most people, and the spectacular view is well worth the effort.

Don't Miss This

Sunsets are phenomenal in Big Bend National Park, and there's no better place to enjoy one than from the Window View Trail (not to be confused with the inaccessible Window Trail). The trailhead is located across the parking lot from the Casa Grande Rooms at Chisos Mountains Lodge, just left of the Basin Store. The trail takes its name from the "window" opening in the canyon that affords a panoramic view of the valley below.

View from the Window View Trail in Big Bend National Park

This .3 mile paved trail offers a gradual descent to the window viewpoint, with benches strategically placed along the route. It's a pleasant place to linger and enjoy views of the spectacular canyon walls and the Chisos Mountains.

Insider Tip

Although it doesn't look like much at first glance, Dugout Wells Picnic Area is the perfect place to enjoy a quiet lunch. Located on the north side of the main road about five miles east of Panther Junction, this secluded picnic area is hidden away behind a wall of dense vegetation that lines the road. To be honest, I discovered it by accident when I stopped to used the accessible vault toilet — the tables are that well hidden.

That said, a level paved path leads from the accessible parking area over to two accessible picnic tables. The tables are set on a cement pad, with plenty of room for wheelchairs at the ends. It's very nicely done, and the surrounding trees provide some welcome shade at the tables. So pick up a hiker's lunch at Chisos Mountain Lodge Restaurant, and enjoy your midday repast at this accessible picnic area.

Picnic table at Dugout Wells Picnic Area in Big Bend National Park

Resources

Big Bend National Park
(432) 477-2251
www.nps.gov/bibe
www.facebook.com/BigBendNPS
twitter.com/BigBendNPS

Forever Resorts (NPS Concessionaire)
(432) 477-2291
www.chisosmountainslodge.com
Chisos Mountains Lodge

View from the Santa Elena Overlook in Big Bend National Park

Utah

Towers of the Virgin in Zion National Park

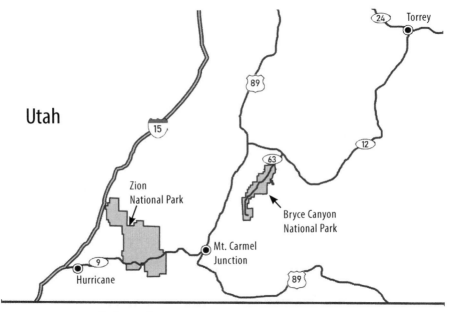

Bryce Canyon National Park

Named for Ebenezer Bryce, a Scottish immigrant who settled in the Paria Valley in 1875, Bryce Canyon National Park is known for the spire-like hoodoos that seem to magically rise from the canyon floor. Created by a combination of freezing, thawing and erosion, these unusual limestone formations were sculpted over millions of years. Today, Bryce Canyon is often described as a cave without a ceiling; as the hoodoos bear a striking resemblance to stalagmites found on cavern floors. And the great thing about Bryce Canyon is, you'll get an entirely different view of these unique formations, as you take a gander at them from the various viewpoints and overlooks throughout the park. Add in a new accessible shared use path and a nicely accessible lodge, and you have an excellent choice for wheelchair-users and slow walkers.

The main park entrance is located on Highway 63, south of Bryce Canyon City; however a short section of Highway 12 also runs through a small northern section of the park.

Although the park is open all year, there may be temporary road closures after snow storms, until the roads are cleared. The road to Fairyland Point is closed to vehicle traffic in the winter, and at times Rainbow Point Road is closed past the Bryce Point turnoff. Additionally, the road out to Paria View is not plowed. It's a good idea to always carry chains or cables when traveling through the park; and keep in mind that late spring snow storms are not uncommon.

There is one lodge in Bryce Canyon National Park.

Admission

$35 – seven-day pass
$40 – yearly pass

Spend the Night

The Lodge at Bryce Canyon

Highway 63
Bryce Canyon, Utah 84764
(877) 386-4383
www.brycecanyonforever.com

Opened in 1925, The Lodge at Bryce Canyon is one of the architectural treasures of our national parks. This rustic lodge was the brainchild of Gilbert Stanley Underwood who also designed Old Faithful Lodge at Yellowstone National Park, the Ahwahnee at Yosemite National Park and Jackson Lake Lodge at Grand Teton National Park. And although modern comforts and access features have been added over the years, this grand old gem still retains the look and feel of yesteryear.

There's accessible parking on the non-canyon side of the lodge, with level access over to the main building. Inside, there's plenty of room to roll around the stately old lobby. Accessible restrooms are located down the hallway on the left side of the front desk.

The new Bryce Canyon Shared Use Path runs in front of the canyon-side of the lodge, with ramp access to the front porch on the right side. Although there are some guest rooms on the second floor of the lodge, there's no elevator in this historic building, so those rooms won't work for wheelchair-users and slow walkers. That said, there are four accessible rooms in the nearby Sunrise and Sunset buildings, which are just a short walk away from the main lodge.

All of the accessible rooms have wide doorways and good pathway access, with level access to the back decks. Accessible parking is available in nearby lots, with level access to the buildings. Additionally, all of the accessible rooms are located on the ground floor.

Room 120, which is located in the Sunset Building, is furnished with two 23-inch high queen-sized beds with wheelchair access on both sides. The spacious bathroom has a roll-in shower with grab bars, a hand-held showerhead and a fold-down shower seat. The toilet grab bars are located on the back and right walls (as seated), and the bathroom also has a roll-under sink.

Room 101 has the same features as room 120, but it is located in the Sunrise Building.

Room 118, which is located in the Sunset Building, is furnished with a 23-inch high king-sized bed with wheelchair access on both sides. The bathroom has a tub/shower combination with grab bars and a hand-held showerhead. The toilet grab bars are located on the back and left walls (as seated), and the bathroom also has a roll-under sink. A portable shower chair is available upon request.

Room 115 has the same features as room 118, but it is located in the Sunrise Building.

The lodge also has a number of duplex and four-plex cabins that are not accessible, but they may be usable for some slow walkers. Each unit is furnished with two 26-inch high beds, a refrigerator, a microwave and a gas fireplace; and they all have a spacious front porch. There are no access features in the cabins, and the bathrooms are equipped with standard tub/shower combination units; however portable shower chairs are available upon request. Most of the cabins have a step or two up to the front porch, but Cabin 515 has level access, so it's a good option for folks who don't need any other access features. These units also feature connecting rooms, so they are a good choice for families or for people who travel with a caregiver.

There's barrier-free access to all the public areas of the lodge, including the bookstore and the restaurant, which are located just off the lobby.

The Lodge at Bryce Canyon is open from late March to early November.

Cabin 515 at The Lodge at Bryce Canyon

Inside of cabin 515 at The Lodge at Bryce Canyon

Bathroom in cabin 515 at The Lodge at Bryce Canyon

Access Overview

There's no shortage of accessible windshield views in Bryce Canyon National Park, and thanks to a fleet of wheelchair-accessible shuttle buses, slow walkers and wheelchair-users can park their cars and leave the driving to someone else. Most of the viewpoints on the canyon rim feature accessible parking and curb-cut access up to the overlooks. The highest point in the park is Rainbow Point, which has an elevation of 9,115 feet; however most spots along the canyon rim have an elevation of 8,000 to 9,000 feet. The lowest point in the park is Yellow Creek, which is located in the northeast section of the park and has an elevation of 6,620 feet.

The Bryce Amphitheater, which is located near the visitor center, is one of the most visited sections of the park, as it contains many of the well known formations. Over the years the famous pink rock has been chiseled and molded into the trademark hoodoos and castle formations that define this national treasure.

Sunset Point, which is one of the most accessible viewpoints in the Bryce Amphitheater, is a good place to begin your visit. A short paved trail leads out to a viewpoint, which offers a view of the Silent City — a collection of hoodoos and fins in a tight formation. There's also a good view of Thor's Hammer just below the overlook on the northern edge. Bryce Point is also worth a stop in the amphitheater. There's barrier-free access to the lower viewpoint, which offers a commanding view and includes a peek at the scenic grottos which are the result of erosion.

Save some time for a scenic drive along Rainbow Point Road. This 18-mile drive begins just after the main park road branches off to the left to Inspiration Point and Bryce Point. There are a number of scenic overlooks and viewpoints along the way, before the road terminates at Rainbow Point. There's a great view of the park from this overlook; however the 300-foot path to the rim has a slight incline, so some manual wheelchair-users may need assistance. Yovimpa Point can also be accessed from Rainbow Point via a paved trail from the south side of the parking area. It's a short walk, and you'll be rewarded with a spectacular view of the Grand Staircase. There are also benches at the overlook, so you can take a break and enjoy the view.

If you'd like to get a little exercise, then check out the accessible section of the Rim Trail that runs from Sunset Point to Sunrise Point. This half-mile segment winds along the canyon rim, and it's paved and mostly level. The access ends at the approach to Sunrise Point, where there's a sweeping view of the Queens Garden.

The most accessible trail in the park — the Bryce Canyon Shared Use Path — was completed in 2015, Although the primary purpose of this trail is to provide a safer route for cyclists, walkers and joggers, it's also an excellent option for wheelchair-users and slow walkers. The trail begins outside of the park at the shuttle staging area at Ruby's in Bryce Canyon City, and travels 2.4 miles to the park entrance, then continues another 2.6 miles to Inspiration Point. The entire five-mile trail is paved, level and wheelchair-accessible. It also connects with the shuttle system so you can do as much of the trail as you like, then hop on the shuttle to return to your car.

Don't Miss This

Although most folks stop at Farview Point, on the way to Rainbow Point, many people totally overlook Piracy Point, which can be accessed from the Farview Point parking lot. A quarter-mile hard-packed dirt trail begins at the north end of the parking lot and travels through a small forest. Although there are a few bumps and ruts along the way, the trail is pretty wide, so these obstacles are easy to dodge in dry weather. The trail ends at a small overlook that offers sweeping canyon views, and although there is a fence along the rim, a strategically placed cut-out allows wheelchair-users unobstructed views.

Insider Tip

Free shuttle bus transportation through the Bryce Canyon amphitheater is available from April through the end of September; and although cars are allowed along this route, parking is at a premium during the busy summer season, so taking the shuttle bus is the easiest way to see the park. All shuttle buses are lift-equipped and they have wheelchair tie-downs, so take the shuttle to avoid disappointment.

The Bryce Canyon Shuttle also offers free tours to Rainbow Point twice daily, from May to October. The 3.5-hour tours stop at many of the viewpoints along the Rainbow Point Road. Reservations are required and they can be made in person at the Best Western Ruby's Inn or Ruby's Campground, or by calling (435) 834-5290. Reservations can be made up to 24 hours in advance, and unclaimed spaces are available on a first-come basis.

Resources

Bryce Canyon National Park
(435) 834-5322
www.nps.gov/brca
www.facebook.com/BryceCanyonnps
twitter.com/BryceCanyonNPS

Road Conditions
(435) 834-5322

Forever Resorts (NPS Concessionaire)
(877) 386-4383
www.brycecanyonforever.com
www.facebook.com/brycecanyonlodge
The Lodge at Bryce Canyon

Barrier-Free Travel; Utah National Parks for Wheelers and Slow Walkers
www.BarrierFreeUtah.com

Zion National Park

Located in Southwestern Utah, Zion National Park was the Beehive State's first national park. Although it occupies 229 square miles, 84 percent of the park has been designated as a protected wilderness area. That said, there are still many developed areas which have accessible trails and scenic drives. At the top of the list is Zion Canyon, which features the trademark sandstone cliffs which adorn many a postcard and travel brochure. Over on the west side of the park, Kolob Canyons offers a more bucolic view of the Colorado Plateau, while Kolob Terrace Road sports a scenic 24-mile drive, with spectacular windshield views. Finally, the Zion-Mount Carmel Scenic Drive not only offers a number of photo-worthy viewpoints, but it also connects the park with Bryce Canyon National Park.

There are four entrances to Zion National Park.

The South Entrance, which leads directly to Zion Canyon, is located on Highway 9 in Springdale.

The East Entrance is located along Highway 9, 16 miles west of Mount Carmel Junction. This route follows the Zion-Mount Carmel Scenic Drive, and later connects to either Zion Canyon or the South Entrance.

The Kolob Terrace Entrance is located off of Highway 9 in Virgin.

The Kolob Canyon Entrance is located in the remote northwestern corner of the park, near exit 40 on Interstate 15.

Zion National Park is open year-round, however many facilities have reduced operating hours in the winter. Road conditions are subject to change, especially from November to May, when roads may temporarily close due to weather conditions. Updated road conditions can be found on the park's website or Twitter feed. Flash flood warnings are also common in the summer months, so check the weather before you head out for the day.

There is one Lodge in Zion National Park.

Admission

$35 – seven-day pass
$50 – yearly pass

Spend the Night
Zion Lodge

Zion Canyon Scenic Drive
Springdale, UT 84767
(888) 297-2757
www.zionlodge.com

Originally constructed in the 1920s, Zion Lodge was destroyed by a fire in 1966. It was quickly rebuilt, but the new design lacked the rustic appeal of the original structure, so in 1990 the exterior of the lodge was restored to its classic appearance. Today, the property offers five accessible rooms and an accessible cabin. As an added bonus, it's one of the most scenic national park properties around, as it's surrounded by Zion Canyon.

Although personal vehicles are prohibited on Zion Canyon Scenic Drive north of Canyon Junction, lodge guests with confirmed reservations will receive a red parking permit that allows them to drive to the lodge. If you don't receive a permit in the mail, let the ranger at the entrance station know that you are a Zion Lodge guest, and you will receive a red permit. Guests must display the red permit when they drive to and from the lodge,

Room 101 at Zion Lodge

Bathroom in room 101 at Zion Lodge

and when they park in the lodge parking lot. Private vehicles parked at the lodge without a valid permit will be ticketed.

There's level access to the main lodge, with barrier-free access to the front desk, the bookstore and the accessible restrooms. The accessible guestrooms are all located in Building A, which is next door to the main lodge. There's accessible parking in the lot in front of Building A, with a level pathway to the front of the building. There's also an accessible drop-off area in front of Building A. The accessible rooms all have wide doorways, lowered peepholes, lowered clothing rods and good pathway access.

Room 101 is furnished with a 28-inch high king-sized bed with wheelchair access on both sides, a desk with a chair, and an easy chair. There's level access out to the private back patio which features a canyon view, and is furnished with a rocking chair and a patio chair without arms (for easy transfers). The bathroom is equipped with a tub/shower combination with grab bars, a hand-held showerhead and a plastic shower bench. The toilet grab bars are located on the back and right walls (as seated), and the bathroom also has a roll-under sink with an angled mirror.

Room 102, which is located across the hall, has the same features as Room 101, except that the toilet grab bars are located on the back and left walls (as

Room 103 at Zion Lodge

seated), and the room has a front lawn view.

Room 103 is furnished with two 28-inch high queen-sized beds with an access aisle between them, a desk with a chair, and an easy chair. There's level access out to the private back patio which features a canyon view, and it's furnished with a rocking chair and a patio chair without arms (for easy transfers). The bathroom is equipped with a roll-in shower with a fold-down shower bench, grab bars and a hand-held showerhead. The toilet grab bars are located on the back and left walls (as seated), and a plastic shower bench

Bathroom in room 103 at Zion Lodge

is also available. A roll-under sink with an angled mirror is located just outside the bathroom, in a tiled area.

Room 104 has the same features as Room 103, except that it's furnished with a 28-inch high king-sized bed with wheelchair access on both sides. This room also has toilet grab bars on the back and right walls (as seated), and a front lawn view.

Room 108 has the same features as Room 102, except that it's furnished with two 28-inch high queen-sized beds with an access aisle between them.

The rustic cabins, which were saved from the 1966 fire, are more secluded and offer a traditional national park lodging experience. Cabin 529 is located a short walk away from the main lodge. Accessible parking is available directly in front of the cabin, with ramp access up to the front porch. There's a small bench on the front porch, and the cabin features wide doorways, a level threshold and good pathway access. Furnishings include a 27-inch high queen-sized bed with wheelchair access on both sides, a desk with a chair, and two side chairs. The original coal-powered fireplace, which has been converted to propane, enhances the rustic ambiance of the cabin.

The bathroom is equipped with a roll-in shower with a fold-down shower bench, grab bars and a hand-held showerhead. The toilet grab bars are

Cabin 529 at Zion Lodge

Inside cabin 529 at Zion Lodge

Bathroom in cabin 529 at Zion Lodge

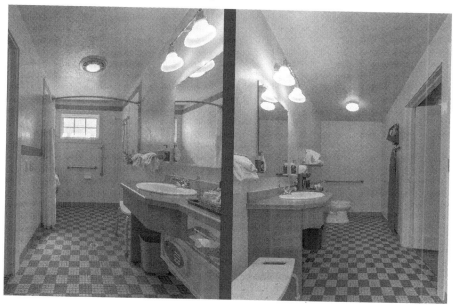

located on the back and left walls (as seated), and the bathroom also includes a roll-under sink and a portable shower bench. Best of all, there's no television in the cabin, so you can just sit back and enjoy the sounds of Mother Nature.

There's barrier-free access to all the public areas at Zion Lodge, including the Red Rock Grill and the Castle Dome Cafe.

Zion Lodge is a popular place to stay, so make plans early to avoid disappointment. Additionally, consider visiting the park during the shoulder season (early spring or late fall) for better lodging availability. Says Operations Manager, Jason Stovall, "November is the best month to visit Zion National Park, as the crowds are gone, the weather is still warm, and the fall colors are absolutely beautiful."

Zion Lodge is open year-round.

Access Overview

The highest point in Zion National Park is Horse Ranch mountain, but Zion Canyon has a more manageable elevation of 4,000 feet. Still, remember to carry plenty of water, and take a break if you start to feel sick. The best way to enjoy Zion Canyon is to hop on a wheelchair-accessible shuttle bus and

Tram used for Zion Canyon Tours

stop at the viewpoints along the drive. Be sure and stop at Weeping Rock Overlook for a look at the hanging gardens created by the dripping springs, and Big Bend Overlook for a view of Angels Landing, The Organ and The Great White Throne.

Accessible open-air tram tours of Zion Canyon are also available. The hour-long tours depart from Zion Lodge in the late afternoon and travel along Zion Canyon Scenic Drive, and feature narration by a local guide. There's ramp access up to the tram, which offers wheelchair and companion seating. Tickets can be purchased at the front desk at Zion Lodge.

Built in the 1920s, the Zion-Mount Carmel Scenic Drive also offers some nice windshield views. The narrow winding road has a number of switchbacks, and there are many pullouts along the way, so you can stop for an extended look at the changing scenery. As you travel along the highway, the red rock canyon slowly transitions to slickrock formations that resemble sand dunes sculpted into the rock, and eventually gives way to white windswept cliffs that mark the east side of the park. The best time to travel this scenic route is in the early morning, as after 8 A.M. there can be delays for large vehicles at the historic Zion-Mount Carmel Tunnel.

The Pa'rus Trail, which is located near the South Entrance, is one of the most accessible trails in the park. This 1.8-mile paved level walkway follows

Pa'rus Trail in Zion National Park

the Virgin River, and runs from the Zion Canyon Visitor Center to Canyon Junction, where you can connect with a shuttle for access to Zion Canyon. Previously a short stretch of the trail at the Canyon Junction end had a steep grade, and was not accessible to manual wheelchair-users; but thanks to some 2019 trail upgrades that access deficit has been fixed. Today the entire length of the trail is wheelchair-accessible.

The Lower Emerald Pool Trail, which is located across from Zion Lodge, may also work for some power wheelchair-users. The .6-mile trail is mostly paved, however the grade is steeper than 1:8 in many places. Additionally, as the trail nears the top, there is a sustained steep grade (up to 20% in places), and there are bumps and breaks in the pavement from continued exposure to the elements. Even if you can't make it to the end, there are still some nice canyon views before you hit the steep section. Alternatively, manual wheelchair-users can get a good canyon view from the bank of the Virgin River, near the trailhead.

Last but not least, make sure and stop at the last shuttle bus stop — The Temple of Sinawava — and take the Riverside Walk. The paved route follows the Virgin River to the beginning of the Zion Narrows, about a mile down the canyon. The first half-mile of the trail is pretty level, but over the years a good deal of dirt has blown over the pavement. As the trail progresses, there are more than a few patches that have a grade steeper than 1:8. Most power

The Virgin River viewed from the start of the Emerald Pools Trail

wheelchair-users will be able to handle the steep sections, but manual wheelchair-users will definitely need some assistance. On the plus side, you can do as much of the trail as you want, then turn back if it's too strenuous for you.

Don't Miss This

The Court of the Patriarchs viewpoint, which is located on Zion Canyon Scenic Drive, offers some great views of the Abraham, Isaac and Jacob peaks (the patriarchs), as well as Mount Moroni and the Sentinel. Although the trail up to the viewpoint is not accessible due to the steep grade, you'll get a good view of the formations from the shuttle bus stop across the street. Additionally, there's a service road just to the right of the down-canyon shuttle bus stop, that leads back to the stables. It's a short walk to the end of the road, where you'll get another good view of the patriarchs. And because this viewpoint isn't mentioned in any park brochures, you'll likely have it all to yourself.

Riverside Walk in Zion National Park

Insider Tip

Free ranger-led tours of Zion Canyon are offered twice daily on the accessible park shuttle buses. These narrated tours last for two hours and include several stops along the Zion Canyon Scenic Drive. There is no charge for the tours, but reservations must be made in person at the Zion Canyon Visitor Center. Seating is limited and reservations may be made up to three days in advance.

Resources

Zion National Park
(435) 772-3256
www.nps.gov/zion
www.facebook.com/zionnps
twitter.com/ZionNPS

Xanterra Travel Collection (NPS Concessionaire)
(888) 297-2757
www.zionlodge.com
www.facebook.com/zionlodge
twitter.com/ZionLodges
Zion Lodge

Barrier-Free Travel; Utah National Parks for Wheelers and Slow Walkers
www.BarrierFreeUtah.com

Virginia

The main lodge building at Big Meadows Lodge in Shenandoah National Park

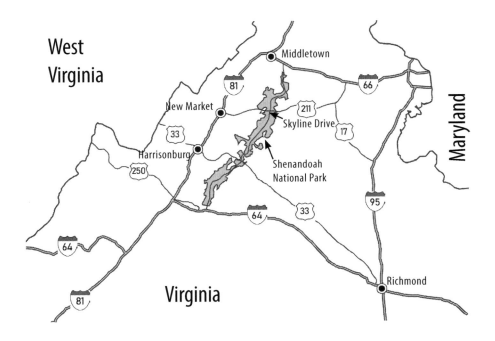

Shenandoah National Park

S henandoah National Park offers the best of both worlds. This Northwestern Virginia refuge is just a short drive from the nation's bustling capitol, yet it's a world away from the trappings of urban life. Filled with cascading waterfalls, wooded hollows and some breathtaking views, the park is a true retreat in every sense of the word. So much so that Herbert Hoover established his own summer sanctuary — Rapidan Camp — there during his presidency.

The park encompasses nearly 200,000 acres of protected lands, including 79,000 acres of wilderness, and a slice of the Appalachian Trail. Skyline Drive crosses the park, and offers some spectacular windshield views along its length. Truly you don't even have to get out of your car to enjoy Shenandoah's majesty; however if you'd like a closer look, there's also a nice selection of accessible overlooks, turnouts and trails.

Shenandoah National Park has four entrances.

The Front Royal Entrance — also known as the North Entrance — is located off Route 340 near the city of Front Royal.

The Thornton Gap Entrance is located just west of Sperryville, along Highway 211.

The Swift Run Gap Entrance is located near milepost 65 of Skyline Drive, southwest of Elkton.

The Rockfish Gap Entrance is located at the south end of the park, two miles east of Waynesboro, off of Highway 250.

It should also be noted that although there are a number of service roads that lead to the park, they are gated and locked, and not open to the public. GPS systems have been known to route visitors to those service roads, so make sure to verify that your GPS directions lead to one of the four official entrances.

Technically the park is open year-round, but portions of Skyline drive are closed during the winter, due to snow, ice and high winds. Road closures are updated on the park website. Most of the park facilities are also closed from November to March.

There are three lodges in Shenandoah National Park.

Admission

$30 – seven-day pass
$55 – yearly pass

Spend the Night

Skyland

Skyland Drive Mile 41.7
Luray, VA 22835
(877) 847-1919
www.goshenandoah.com

Originally known as Stony Mountain Camp, Skyland dates back to 1888. And although there have been a few changes to the property since George Freeman Pollock originally broke ground, the natural beauty of the surrounding forest remains unchanged. Listed on the National Register of Historic Places, this mountain lodge has also added some access upgrades over the years; and today this 178-room property makes an excellent choice for wheelchair-users and slow walkers who want to overnight in Shenandoah National Park.

Room 14 at Skyland

Located near milepost 41, Skyland is the northernmost property in the park. Accessible parking is located near the lodge office, with an accessible cement pathway down to the front door. Accessible room 14 is located near the office, with accessible parking nearby. This large corner room not only offers excellent access, but also boats a lovely valley view.

Access features include wide doorways, wood floors, lever handles, a lowered closet rod, and good pathway access. Furnishings include a 19-inch high open-frame king-sized bed with wheelchair access on both sides, two night tables, a chest of drawers and a table with two chairs. And if you want to catch up on the news, there's also a television in the room.

The bathroom features a full five-foot turning radius, and is equipped with a roll-in shower with grab bars, a hand-held showerhead, and a fold-down padded shower bench. The toilet grab bars are located on the back and right walls (as seated), and the bathroom also has a roll-under sink and a lowered mirror. It's obvious that considerable thought was put into the accessibility of the room, as the shower controls are located within easy reach of the shower seat, and there's also a lowered towel hook near the sink.

And out on the semi-private front porch, there's plenty of room to maneuver even the largest wheelchair or scooter. It's the perfect place to sit back and enjoy the sunset, or to just relax after a busy travel day.

Bathroom in room 14 at Skyland

Access to the public areas of Skyland — which are located next to the office — is equally impressive. There's barrier-free access to the day lodge, with level access over to the Mountain Room taproom, gift shop and grab-and-go food kiosk. Accessible restrooms are located just off the lobby, and there's ramp access down to the main dining room, which also offers a great view of the surrounding forest. Not only is Skyland a great place to spend the night, but it's also a very accessible spot to grab a bite to eat during the day. Additionally it's close to one of the most accessible trails in the park.

Skyland is usually open from late March to late November, weather permitting.

Big Meadows Lodge

Skyline Drive Mile 51.2
Stanley, VA 22851
(877) 847-1919
www.goshenandoah.com

Big Meadows Lodge is hard to miss, as the entrance is located across the street from the namesake meadow on Skyline Drive, near milepost 51. Completed in 1939, the main lodge building is a treasure itself, with wormy chestnut-lined walls, and beams crafted from native oak. Placed on the

Room 95 at Big Meadows Lodge

Bathroom in room 95 at Big Meadows Lodge

National Register of Historic Places in 1997, this rustic mountain retreat offers the ambiance of yesteryear, combined with the amenities and access features of modern times.

There's no permanent parking in front of the main lodge building, but it's possible to parallel park an adapted vehicle in the short-term registration area in front. From there, there's level access on a cement walkway to the main building. Inside there's barrier-free access to the front desk, spacious lobby and large front deck.

Accessible room 95 is located on the bottom floor of the Rapidan Building, which is a short drive away. There's accessible parking near the building, and barrier-free access to the room over an accessible sidewalk. And even though there are many paths in the area, the accessible route is clearly marked.

Access features in the room include wide doorways, lever handles, a lowered peephole, laminate floors, a lowered clothing rod and good pathway access. Furnishings include a 19-inch high open-frame king-sized bed with wheelchair access on both sides, two night tables, a chest of drawers, a table and two chairs, and even a television. There's also access to the adjoining room for an attendant or family member.

The bathroom includes a five-foot turning radius and is equipped with a roll-in shower with grab bars, a hand-held showerhead and a portable shower chair. Round it out with toilet grab bars on the back and left walls (as seated), and a roll-under sink, and you have a nicely accessible room.

There's also level access through the back door to a semi-private cement patio, which offers a peaceful view of the adjacent meadow. And even with the included table and two chairs, there's still room for a wheelchair out there.

There's also barrier-free access to the public spaces at the lodge, including the gift shop which is located next door to the main lodge. The dining room features level access from the adjacent lobby; and even though stairs lead down to the taproom, there's also elevator access from the lobby level. And although some manual wheelchair-users may have problems with the pitch of the sidewalk between the guest rooms and the main lodge, there's also a drop-off area in front. All in all it's a very comfortable, accessible and well-equipped historic mountain lodge.

Big Meadows Lodge is open from early May to early November.

Lewis Mountain Cabins

Skyline Drive Mile 57.5
Elkton, VA 22827
(877) 847-1919
www.goshenandoah.com

Located in the southern end of the park near milepost 57, historic Lewis Mountain Cabins date back to the 1940s. Today these rustic structures offer visitors a comfortable place to overnight, away from the maddening crowds of city life. The accommodations and nearby concessions are pretty basic, but to be honest, that's part of the appeal of these homey cabins.

Accessible parking is located in front of the nearby camp store, which also serves as the cabin registration office. There's barrier-free access to the store, which carries a good selection of grocery items, camping supplies and souvenirs. It's just a short level drive or walk from the store over to cabin 13, the accessible unit.

Parking is available on a level asphalt pad in front of the cabin, with ramp access to the front porch. Although the cabin itself is quite roomy and accessible, the accessible picnic table on the front porch may present an obstacle to some folks — especially power wheelchair-users. Generally, as placed, it allows for 26 inches of clearance to the front door; however the folks at Lewis Mountain Cabins are very accommodating, so make

Bedroom 1 at Lewis Mountain Cabins, cabin 13

sure you let them know if you need the table moved when you make your reservation.

Access features in the two-bedroom cabin include, wide doorways, wood floors, lever handles and lowered closet rods. One bedroom is furnished

Bedroom 2 at Lewis Mountain Cabins, cabin 13

Bathroom in cabin 13 at Lewis Mountain Cabins

with a 24-inch high queen-sized bed with wheelchair access on the right side (as you face it), and a chest of drawers. That said, there's plenty of room in the spacious bedroom to move the bed if you require access on the other side. The other bedroom is equally spacious and is also furnished with a 24-inch high queen-sized bed, with a 30-inch access aisle on the right side (as you face it), when the bed is pushed up against the left wall. Other furnishings include a chest of drawers and two wooden chairs.

The bathroom features a full five-foot turning radius, and is equipped with a tub/shower combination with grab bars, a hand-held showerhead, and a portable shower chair. Other access features include toilet grab bars on the back and right walls (as seated), a roll-under sink and a lowered mirror.

Guests are welcome to bring along a camp stove, but there's also a charcoal grill near the front porch. There's no refrigerator in the cabin, so you'll also have to pack along an ice chest if you want to prepare your own meals. And if you want to leave the cooking to someone else, you can always dine at Skyland or Big Mountain Lodge, both of which have accessible full-service restaurants. Either way, this comfortable mountain cabin offers a pleasant spot to stop and smell the roses — or the mountain laurel — in Shenandoah National Park.

Lewis Mountain Cabins are open from mid-March to late November.

Access Overview

The best way to get a good overview of the varied landscape of the park is to drive along Skyline Drive. This 105-mile drive is an accessible window on nature, with excellent views along the way. For the best views take the route from north to south, as the low Civilian Conservation Corps walls along the west side of the road offer unobstructed views. That said, there are certainly a number of accessible pullouts along the way to stop and take a photo or two. This route also makes a beautiful fall foliage drive.

Skyline Drive starts out at an elevation of 712 feet at the Front Royal Entrance, and climbs to the high point of 3,680 feet near Skyland. After that, the road winds slowly down to 3,535 feet at Big Meadows, and 3,441 feet at Lewis Mountain, before it ends at 1,900 feet at the Rockfish Gap Entrance. The highest point in the park — only reachable on foot — is Hawksbill Mountain, with an elevation of 4,050 feet.

There's also a short accessible trail at the Dickey Ridge Visitor Center. There's plenty of accessible parking near the visitor center, with barrier-free access around to the back of the building. The short paved trail is just 50 feet long, and it leads to an accessible overlook with an expansive view. It's also a favorite stop for tour buses.

Limberlost Trail in Shenandoah National Park

Finally, make sure and check out the Limberlost Trail, located near Skyland. There's accessible parking near the trailhead with level access over to the hard-packed dirt trail covered with decomposed granite. The 1.3-mile trail begins with a walk through a wooded area filled with oaks, ferns and mountain laurels, before it transitions to a wetlands boardwalk, and finally crosses the river and loops back to the beginning. It's especially beautiful in June, when the mountain laurels are in bloom.

Don't Miss This

A visit to Herbert Hoover's Rapidan Camp, is a must-do on any Shenandoah visit. That said, you need to plan ahead for this popular tour. Private vehicles are prohibited along the road to this former camp, but special wheelchair-accessible tours are available. These tours are conducted in accessible vehicles, twice daily on Thursday, Friday, Saturday and Sunday, from late May to late October. The accessible tours are conducted at 10:00 a.m. and 2:00 p.m.

The 2.5-hour tours begin at the Harry F. Byrd, Sr. Visitor Center at milepost 51 on Skyline Drive. It's about a half-hour drive to the camp, which features the President's 1929 Cabin (also known as the Brown House), the Prime Minister's Cabin and The Creel (a smaller cabin). Once passengers arrive, they are given a ranger-led tour, which offers some good insight on both the president and the era.

Visitors can make reservations for the accessible tours at www.recreation. gov, up to six months in advance. Reservations cannot be made in person, so get your tickets early to avoid disappointment.

Insider Tip

Shenandoah National Park is noted for its night skies, so make plans to attend one of the evening astronomy programs on your visit. These free programs are held at milepost 51, right outside the Rapidian Camp gate, on select Fridays during the summer. Amateur astronomers present a short program on the prevention of light pollution, and then visitors are invited to gaze at the heavens through telescopes. The programs are presented in a flat level area, but don't forget to bring along a blanket and a flashlight. Best of all, there's no charge for these excellent programs.

Resources

Shenandoah National Park

(540) 999-3500

www.nps.gov/shen

www.facebook.com/shenandoahnps

twitter.com/ShenandoahNPS

Road Conditions

(540) 999-3500

Delaware North (NPS Concessionaire)

(877) 847-1919

www.goshenandoah.com

www.facebook.com/ShenandoahNationalParkLodging/

twitter.com/GoShenandoahNP

Skyland

Big Meadows Lodge

Lewis Mountain Cabins

Washington

Glines Canyon Spillway Overlook in Olympic National Park

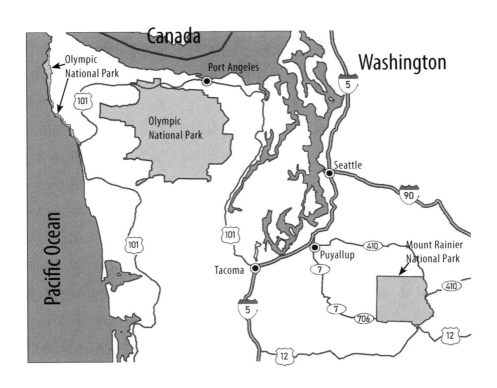

Olympic National Park

Located on the Olympic Peninsula, Olympic National Park occupies nearly one million acres brimming with sub-alpine forests, wildflower-filled meadows, lush rainforests and rugged coastal bluffs. From the heights of Hurricane Ridge to the peaceful shores of Lake Crescent, and the natural hot springs at Sol Duc, you have a park that's as diverse as it is massive. And although a good portion of this park is rugged backcountry, major access improvements have been made to the trails and lodgings in the developed areas, making this Washington national park a good choice for wheelchair-users and slow walkers.

Highway 101 circumnavigates Olympic National Park and provides numerous access points.

Up north in Port Angeles, Highway 101 passes Race Street, which leads to the main park visitor center. From the visitor center, Hurricane Ridge Road continues south and enters the park near Heart O' the Hills, and later dead ends up at Hurricane Ridge.

Highway 101 continues west from Port Angeles, passes the turnoff to Elwha and enters the park near Lake Crescent. The highway then continues west along the lakeshore, past the turnoff to Sol Duc, before it exits the park.

The highway then turns south and passes the turnoff to the Hoh Rain Forest, as it continues on through the Olympic Wilderness. Highway 101 reenters the park near Ruby Beach, continues south through Kalaloch, then exits the park and heads east.

Finally the highway skirts the south border of the park, passes the turnoff to the Quinault Rain Forest, then heads south towards Aberdeen.

Olympic National Park is open year-round. The Olympic National Park Visitor Center in Port Angeles is also open all year, but the regional visitor centers are closed or have reduced days and hours from September to May. Road closures are possible at any time due to heavy snow in the winter months.

Highway 101 is open year-round, but Hurricane Ridge Road closes for snow removal, and sometimes when it's actively snowing. All vehicles are required to carry tire chains or cables when they travel on Hurricane Ridge Road above Heart O' the Hills from November 15 to April 1. Olympic Hot Springs Road (near Elwha) is prone to flooding and washouts during heavy rains. Sol Duc Hot Springs Road also closes seasonally due to weather. Updated road conditions are available on the park website and social media accounts.

There are four lodges in Olympic National Park.

Admission
$30 – seven-day pass
$55 – yearly pass

Spend the Night
Lake Crescent Lodge

416 Lake Crescent Road
Port Angeles, WA 98363
(888) 896-3818
www.olympicnationalparks.com

Located on the south shore of Lake Crescent, this historic property dates back to 1915. The main lodge building is the focal point of the property, with additional guest rooms and cabins dotted throughout the surrounding

Lake Crescent Lodge

Room 101 at Lake Crescent Lodge

old growth forest. And although Lake Crescent Lodge is the oldest property in the park, access upgrades — including the addition of the lakeside Marymere wing — have been added over the years.

There's accessible parking near the main lodge with barrier-free access to the front lobby. From there it's just a short roll on a paved sidewalk over to the Marymere building. Room 101, which is located on the end, features wide doorways and good pathway access. It's furnished with two 24-inch high queen-sized beds, with wheelchair access on all sides.

Bathroom in room 101 at Lake Crescent Lodge

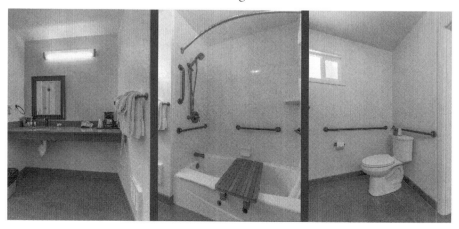

The bathroom includes a full five-foot turning radius, and is equipped with a tub/shower combination with grab bars, a hand-held showerhead and a wooden shower bench. The toilet grab bars are located on the back and right walls (as seated), and the bathroom also has a roll-under sink. A plastic shower chair is available upon request.

There is a slight 3/4-inch lip at the back door, which leads out to a shared porch that's furnished with two chairs. Although there's plenty of room to maneuver a wheelchair, you can always move the chairs if the space is too tight. It's the perfect place to sit back and enjoy the beautiful alpine lake.

Room 102, which is located next door, has the same access features.

The Pyramid Mountain Rooms, which are located across the parking lot, offer a forest setting and a nice meadow view. Room 300 in the Pyramid Building is not flagged as an accessible room, but it may work for some slow walkers.

There's accessible parking near the room with level access over to the front door. The room features wide doorways, good pathway access, a lowered peephole and a lowered clothing rod. It's furnished with a 25-inch high queen-sized platform bed with wheelchair access on both sides, two large easy chairs, a small table and two bedside tables.

The bathroom has a full five-foot turning radius and is equipped with a tub/

Room 300 in the Pyramid Rooms building at Lake Crescent Lodge

Bathroom in room 300 in the Pyramid Rooms building at Lake Crescent Lodge

shower combination with grab bars. There is no hand-held showerhead; and although there is a fold-down shower bench installed at the far end of the tub, the bottom of the bench is a full 10-12 inches above the top of the tub. It can however, be folded up out of the way; and a plastic shower chair is available upon request. Other bathroom access features include a toilet with grab bars on the back and left walls (as seated), and a roll-under sink with a lowered mirror.

There's also level access out the back door to a small semi-private patio; however one of the easy chairs may have to be moved for optimal pathway access. This corner room is a bit farther from the lake than the Marymere rooms, but it still has a partial lake view. And it's certainly spacious enough to accommodate a wheelchair or even a large scooter. It's important to note though, that since this room isn't listed in the accessible room inventory, it needs to be specifically requested in the reservation.

The Singer Tavern Cottages may also work for some slow walkers. They don't have any access features, but they are located close to the main lodge.

There's barrier-free access to all of the public areas in the main lodge building, including the restaurant and the popular glassed-in porch. There's no wheelchair access to the second floor of this former tavern, where historic lodge rooms with shared bathrooms are located.

Lake Crescent Lodge is open from late April to early January.

Sol Duc Hot Springs Resort

12076 Sol Duc Hot Springs Road
Port Angeles, WA 98363
(888) 896-3818
www.olympicnationalparks.com

Located along the Sol Duc River, south of Lake Crescent, Sol Duc Hot Springs Resort features refreshing hot springs pools, and offers overnight accommodations in rustic cabins. Accessible parking is located near the office, with ramp access up to the front door.

Cabin 132 is located just a short drive away, with accessible parking available in back. There's ramp access from the parking area up to the cabin, which features a wide doorway and good pathway access.

The cozy cabin is furnished with two 28-inch high double beds with an access aisle between them, an easy chair and a dining table with two chairs. The bathroom is equipped with a tub/shower combination with grab bars. There is also a roll-under sink in the bathroom, but the toilet lacks grab bars.

There's level access to a large grassy area in front of the cabin, which features a picnic table. There is also plenty of room to roll around on the front porch, which is furnished with a small bench.

Bedroom in cabin 132 at Sol Duc Hot Springs Resort

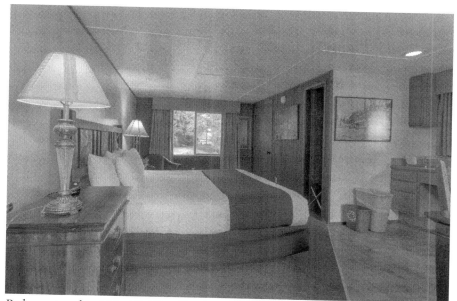

Bedroom in cabin 111 at Sol Duc Hot Springs Resort

Kitchen in cabin 111 at Sol Duc Hot Springs Resort

Cabin 133, which is located next door has the same access features as Cabin 132.

Cabin 111, which is located across the parking lot, features accessible parking with ramp access to the front deck. Access features include wide doorways and low-pile carpet for easy rolling. Furnishings include a 23-inch high king-sized bed with wheelchair-access on both sides, two night stands, an easy chair, and a dining table with two chairs. The cabin also includes a kitchenette with a microwave, stove, and a full-size refrigerator. The sink features roll-under access, and the kitchenette includes dishes, pots and utensils.

Like Cabin 132, this unit is also equipped with a bathroom with a tub/shower combination with grab bars and a roll-under sink. There's also level access to the grassy common area in front of the cabin, with barrier-free access to a picnic table.

There's barrier-free access to all the public areas of the property, including the hot springs pools and the Springs Restaurant, which are located near the office.

Sol Duc Hot Springs Resort is open from March to October.

Bathroom in cabin 111 at Sol Duc Hot Springs Resort

Log Cabin Resort

3183 E. Beach Road
Port Angeles, WA 98363
(888) 896-3818
www.olympicnationalparks.com

Located on the north shore of Lake Crescent, Log Cabin Resort is the second property to occupy the site. Log Cabin Hotel was previously erected on the lakeshore in 1895, but it was later destroyed in a fire in 1932. Log Cabin Resort replaced the hotel in the early 1950s, after the former national monument was re-designated as a national park in 1938.

There's accessible parking in front of the lodge, with level access to the registration desk. Two new accessible cabins — which are located a short drive away — were added in 2018, as part of a $2 million renovation project.

Access features include accessible parking next to the cabins with barrier-free access over to the accessible units (1c and 2c). Inside there's good pathway access, and both units have an accessible bathroom that's equipped with a roll-in shower with a built-in shower bench, a toilet with grab bars, and a roll-under sink. One of the accessible units also includes a kitchenette.

Units 1c and 2c at Log Cabin Resort

There's also an accessible picnic table in front of each unit, and since the cabins are located on a hill above the main lodge they also offer excellent lake views.

There is barrier-free access to the public areas of the resort, including the Sunnyside Café, the gift shop, snack bar and the dock. There's also a level sidewalk that leads from the parking lot to the lakeshore side of the property.

Log Cabin Resort is open from late May to late September.

Kalaloch Lodge

157151 Highway 101
Forks, WA 98331
(866) 662-9928
www.thekalalochlodge.com

Located along the rugged Pacific coast, Kalaloch Lodge offers rustic but comfortable accessible cabins, and spectacular ocean views. Accessible parking is available in front of the main building, and there is ramp access to the front door. There are steps down into the adjacent gift shop, which also doubles as the office; however, there is level access to the gift shop via a sliding glass door in the back. Just head to the left of the building from the accessible parking spot.

Great room in cabin 40 at Kalaloch Lodge

Kitchen in cabin 40 at Kalaloch Lodge

Cabin 40, which is located near the office, features reserved parking in a large level area. The parking space isn't striped, but there's plenty of room for an accessible van to deploy the ramp. There's ramp access up to the front door of this duplex cabin, which features wide doorways and good pathway access.

Bedroom in cabin 40 at Kalaloch Lodge

The large kitchen has a roll-under counter and it's equipped with a refrigerator, stove, microwave and a coffee maker. There are plenty of pots, pans, dishes and glasses, and the kitchen also has a roll-under sink. The dining table has four bar chairs, and there is additional bar seating at the kitchen counter. The living room has an 18-inch high double futon, two easy chairs and a wood burning stove. There is also a coffee table in front of the futon, which makes this a good accessible place to enjoy a meal by the fire.

The adjacent bedroom is furnished with two 30-inch high queen-sized beds with an access aisle between them. There is a wide doorway into the bathroom which has a full five-foot turning radius and is equipped with a large roll-in shower (six feet wide, and four feet deep) with grab bars, a hand-held showerhead and a portable shower chair. The toilet has a grab bar on the right side (as seated), and there is also a roll-under sink with a lowered mirror in the bathroom. They even remembered the small access touches, like lowered robe hooks and a lowered soap dispenser.

Outside there's an accessible picnic table on a level grassy spot. And if you'd like to explore the area, the cabin is equipped with some walking sticks and a pair of binoculars.

Cabin 43, which is rated as "partially accessible", is a bluff view cabin. It has the same basic furnishings and access features as cabin 40, except that it has a 36-inch square transfer-type shower, with a built-in shower seat in

Bathroom in cabin 40 at Kalaloch Lodge

the back corner. You have to be able to take a step in order to use this unit because of the shower lip. Additionally the toilet grab bars are located on the back and left walls (as seated).

There's a gazebo that overlooks the beach near Cabin 43, that has an accessible parking space next to it. There's a small bump up to the gazebo, but it's manageable with a little assistance. Alternatively there's level access to picnic tables on the adjacent grassy area, which offer equally stunning ocean views.

There's barrier-free access to all of the public areas of the property as well, including the restaurant, mercantile, gift shop and lobby.

Kalaloch Lodge is open year-round.

Access Overview

Filled with rain forests, hot springs and alpine lakes, Olympic National Park offers a good variety of accessible trails and scenic drives. Truly one of the most accessible ways to experience the park is to drive around and enjoy the windshield views, and stop at the scenic overlooks and pullouts along the way. Some of the picnic areas even offer breathtaking mountain or lake views. The highest point in the park is Mount Olympus with an elevation of 7,965 feet; however it's located in a wilderness area. Elevations vary greatly

Living Forest Trail in Olympic National Park

in the developed areas of the park, from sea level on the coastal section, to 580 feet at Lake Crescent and 5,242 feet at Hurricane Ridge.

The Living Forest Trail, which is located behind the Olympic National Park Visitor Center in Port Angeles, is a good choice for wheelchair-users and slow walkers. This hard-packed dirt trail, which is covered in crushed granite, leads through the forest and features a nice view of Peabody Creek Valley. The trail is fairly level, with the steepest grade being near the beginning. Generally the trail is wide, although it narrows to about 28-inches in a few places; and there's a bench to sit and take a break about half-way along this .6-mile trail. And since the trail is shaded by the forest, it makes a good choice on a hot day.

One of the most popular accessible trails in the park — the Moments in Time Nature Trail — is located a short walk from Lake Crescent Lodge. The .8-mile hard packed dirt trail winds through the mature forest and around some old homestead sites; and although it's rated as "accessible with assistance", it's doable for most wheelchair-users and slow walkers.

Madison Falls, which is located on Olympic Hot Springs Road near Elwha, is also worth a visit. A .1-mile paved level trail leads through the forest to the base of Madison Falls, where you'll find an accessible overlook with lowered railings for unobstructed views. There's also a bench for slow walkers who want to linger on and enjoy the view.

Glines Canyon Spillway Overlook, which is located at the end of Olympic Hot Springs Road, offers an interesting perspective on the result of the Elwha Dam Restoration Project. This massive undertaking began in September 2011 with the removal of the Elwha and Glines Canyon Dams on the Elwha River. There's level access to the Glines Canyon Spillway Overlook, which leads out over the top of the former spillway. Interpretive panels and audio kiosks dot the short path to the overlook, but the big attraction of this site is the view down into the river.

Up on Hurricane Ridge, some power wheelchair-users may be able to access two of the meadow trails. The Cirque Rim Trail and the Big Meadow Loop, which are located near the visitor center, are paved; but the first 100-foot stretch that leads out to the rim overlook has a grade greater than 1:8. If you can make it up the first hill, turn right at the overlook and follow the Cirque Rim Trail for a half-mile, then loop back on the Big Meadow Loop segment for another quarter-mile. The trails are fairly level and they offer sweeping views of Port Angeles, the Juan de Fuca Strait and the Olympic Mountains.

Named for the Native Americans that originally inhabited the area, the Hoh Rain Forest also has a few doable trails. The Mini Rain Forest Trail begins on the back porch of the visitor center. This quarter-mile flat paved trail winds through the old growth forest before it loops back to the parking lot. The trailhead to the Hall of Mosses Trail is located at the .1-mile point along the Mini Rain Forest Trail. This hard-packed dirt trail is level and doable for about 75 yards. Once you hit the bridge the trail loses its access, as the grade gets steeper and there are steps along the way. Still it's a nice stroll through the rainforest, and you can even spot salmon in the river during the fall.

Over in Lake Quinault, there are a few longer trails near the Quinault Rain Forest Ranger Station. The Maple Glade Trail is a half-mile hard-packed dirt trail that starts near the ranger station and either connects to the Kastner Homestead Trail, or loops back to the trailhead. The trail is fairly level, but there are a few bumps here and there, and it narrows to about two-feet in a few places. It's a pleasant stroll under the forest canopy, with boardwalk areas over the damp areas along the route.

The trailhead for the Kestner Homestead Trail is also located near the picnic area at the Quinault Rain Forest Ranger Station. This 1.3-mile hard-packed dirt trail is covered in crushed granite and is fairly level. It winds through the forest and crosses a bridge, before it passes through the abandoned homestead. There's a level path around the homestead, which is littered with some old farm buildings and vintage equipment. The trail then continues

Kestner Homestead in Olympic National Park

back through the forest, passes the Maple Glade Trail, and returns to the trailhead. There are some large pieces of gravel on the two-to-three foot wide trail, but for the most part they are easy to avoid.

Don't Miss This

One of the most accessible trails in the park — The Spruce Railroad Trail — follows the grade of the historic railroad, which was abandoned in 1951. A five-mile section of this former rail bed is now paved and mostly wheelchair-accessible.

The access begins at the North Shore Picnic Area on the west side, which is located along Camp David Jr. Road. From there it follows the Lake Crescent shore to the Spruce Railroad Trailhead. After that it's a one-mile walk to the Daley Rankin Tunnel, then a 1.6 mile walk to the McPhee Tunnel, and another 1.1 mile walk to the Lyre River Trailhead on the east side. The trail is wide, mostly level and paved along this accessible length. The one exception is near the Lyre River Trailhead (noted below).

The Lyre Rive Trailhead is located at the end of Boundary Creek Road, next to Log Cabin Resort. There is a paved parking lot next to the trailhead, and although the trail conforms to access standards, this trailhead does not

The Spruce Railroad Trail in Olympic National Park

have level access. Power wheelchair-users and scooter-users will have no problems with the grade, but manual wheelchair-users will need substantial assistance for the first quarter-mile. After that the trail levels out and follows the shore of Lake Crescent.

It should be noted, that at press time there was still some minor construction along the accessible length of the trail, but it is expected to be completed by Summer 2020. Check the park website for construction updates.

Insider Tip

Save some time to stop and take the waters at Sol Duc Hot Springs, which features excellent access. There's ramp access to the Sol Duc Hot Springs front office, with barrier-free access to the pools in back. The pool area features good pathway access, and the complex also includes barrier-free changing rooms and accessible restrooms. The mineral wading pool is reserved for children under three, but the Large Mineral Fountain Pool (101°) and the Freshwater Pool (50°- 80°, depending on the season) feature ramp access. There is also a portable pool lift available for these pools or for the Medium Mineral Pool (104°), which isn't ramped. Admission to the pools is free for Sol Duc Hot Springs Resort guests, but others can purchase a day-use pass. A loaner wheelchair is also available on a first-come basis.

The Large Mineral Fountain Pool at Sol duc Hot Springs

And while you're on the way to the hot springs stop along Sol Duc Road to see the Salmon Cascades. A hard-packed dirt trail leads from the accessible parking area out to the Salmon Cascades overlook. The trail is wide and level and doable for most folks. The best time to spot the salmon leaping over the falls is in the fall, but it's still a scenic stop the rest of the year.

Resources

Olympic National Park
(360) 565-3130
www.nps.gov/olym
www.facebook.com/OlympicNPS
twitter.com/OlympicNP

Road Conditions
(360) 565-3131

Aramark (NPS Concessionaire)
(888) 896-3818
www.olympicnationalparks.com
www.facebook.com/olympicnationalpark/
Lake Crescent Lodge
Sol Duc Hot Springs Resort
Log Cabin Resort

Delaware North (NPS Concessionaire)
(866) 662-9928
www.thekalalochlodge.com
www.facebook.com/KalalochLodge/
twitter.com/KalalochLodge
Kalaloch Lodge

Barrier-Free Travel; Washington National Parks for Wheelers and Slow Walkers
www.BarrierFreeOlympic.com

Mount Rainier National Park

L ocated 100 miles southeast of Seattle, Mount Rainier National Park is situated in one of the most rugged areas of Washington State. At 14,410 feet, the namesake mountain towers over the park; and not only is this active volcano the most glaciated peak in the contiguous US, but it's also a popular climb, with over 10,000 attempts each year. That said, you can certainly enjoy the park without attempting the summit, as there are also several developed areas that offer accessible trails, museums and overnight lodging.

There are five entrances to Mount Rainier National Park, four of which can be accessed by a vehicle.

The Nisqually Entrance is located on the southwest corner of the park, and it's the only vehicle entrance that's open year-round. It's located about 1.5-hours southeast of Tacoma.

The Carbon River Entrance is located in the northwest corner of the park, about 2 hours southeast of Seattle. This entrance is only open to bicycles and pedestrians.

The Stevens Canyon Entrance is located on Highway 123 in the southeast section of the park, just north of   .

The Chinook Pass Entrance is located on the east side of the park, about 1.5 hours northwest of Yakima on Highway 410.

The White River Entrance is located along the road to Sunrise and can be accessed from Highway 410, which runs through the park.

Although the park is open year-round most of the entrances close seasonally due to harsh weather. Even the Nisqually Entrance, which is open year-round, can close after a heavy snow.

The road from Longmire to Paradise usually closes in the evenings beginning in November, but it may reopen in the morning depending on weather conditions. The road to Sunrise closes every night, beginning in late September, and opens the following morning if weather conditions permit. The whole road closes after the first heavy snowfall, which can be as early as October 1.

Conditions can change quickly during the winter months, so it's best to check with park headquarters before you travel. Updates on road conditions can also be found on the park's Twitter feed.

Additionally, vehicles are required to carry tire chains or cables from November 1 to May 1. This applies to all vehicles — even four-wheel drive vehicles and trucks with snow tires — regardless of the weather conditions.

There are two lodges in Mount Rainier National Park.

Admission
$30 – seven-day pass
$55 – yearly pass

Spend the Night
National Park Inn

17009 Paradise Road East
Ashford, WA 98304
(360) 569-2275
www.mtrainierguestservices.com

Built in 1906, The National Park Inn proved stiff competition for the nearby Longmire Medical Springs property; and although they enjoyed a healthy

The National Park Inn at Longmire

Bedroom in room 2 at The National Park Inn at Longmire

rivalry for twenty years, both properties were destroyed in a 1926 fire. Fortunately the inn annex survived the inferno, and today this historic building houses the 25-room National Park Inn.

There's accessible parking near the entrance, with level access to the front lobby. Room 2, which is the most accessible room at the inn, is located just around the corner.

Bathroom in room 2 at The National Park Inn at Longmire

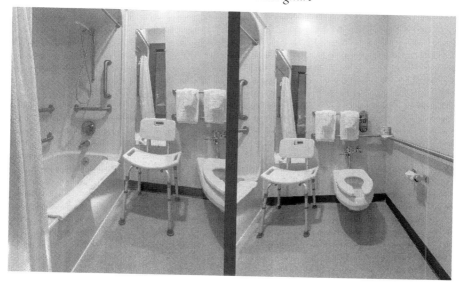

The room features wide doorways and it's furnished with a 26-inch high queen-sized bed with wheelchair access on the right side (as you face it). There is a wide pocket door into the bathroom, which is equipped with a tub/shower combination with a hand-held showerhead and a portable shower bench. The toilet grab bars are located on the back and left walls (as seated), and there is a roll-under sink right outside the bathroom.

There's barrier-free access to the public areas of the inn, including the lobby, restaurant and study. There is also level access to the spacious back porch, where you can enjoy an adult beverage and take in the Mount Rainier view.

The National Park Lodge is open year-round.

Paradise Inn

52807 Paradise Road East
Mount Rainier National Park, WA 98368
(360) 569-2275
www.mtrainierguestservices.com

Built in 1916, the Paradise Inn is one of the few surviving grand old national park lodges. After falling into disrepair the property was slated for demolition, but a vocal protest from an adoring public saved it from the wrecking ball. Finally in 1979, the National Park Service spent $1.75 million to replace the failing foundation and repair the existing walls. Today this 121-room inn once again welcomes guests from around the world.

Paradise Inn in Mount Rainier National Park

Bedroom in room 331 at Paradise Inn in Mount Rainier National Park

Accessible parking is available in front of the inn, with level access to the front lobby. Room 331, which is located on the lobby level, features wide doorways and good pathway access. It's furnished with two 27-inch high double beds with an access aisle between them, a desk and a chair, a chest of drawers and a nightstand.

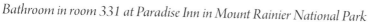
Bathroom in room 331 at Paradise Inn in Mount Rainier National Park

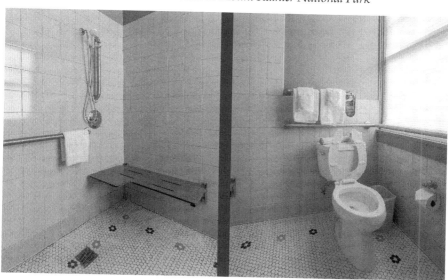

The bathroom is equipped with a roll-in shower with grab bars, a hand-held showerhead and a portable shower chair. Although the five-foot turning radius extends into the shower, there's still plenty of room to maneuver a wheelchair. The toilet grab bars are located on the back and left walls (as seated); and there's a roll-under sink in the bedroom, in order to free-up more bathroom floor space.

There's good wheelchair access to all the public areas of the inn, including the lobby, gift shop and restaurants. An accessible family restroom is located just off the lobby, and the men's and women's restrooms both have accessible stalls. The massive lobby is reminiscent of those grand old lodges of yesteryear, and it's the perfect place to curl up with a good book.

The Paradise Inn is open from mid-May to October.

Access Overview

Variety is the key word in Mount Rainier National Park — in the landscape, scenery and the altitude. The lowest elevation — just 1,600 feet — is found near the old growth forest in Ohanapecosh, in the southeast corner of the park. Longmire, on the other hand has an elevation of 2,761 feet, and Paradise clocks in at an impressive 5,400 feet. Sunrise, which is the highest elevation reachable by vehicle, has an elevation of 6,400 feet — and a spectacular view of the Cascades.

The Kautz Creek Trail in Mount Rainier National Park

Indeed, one of the most accessible things to do in the park is to take the 56-mile scenic drive from Longmire to Sunrise. Although the drive takes about two-and-a-half hours straight through, it's best to allow a whole day for it, as you'll want to stop and enjoy the views along the way, as well as spend some time on top. And although the windshield views are breathtaking on the drive up, they are even more spectacular on the trip back down the hill.

The Kautz Creek Trail, which is located near the Nisqually Entrance, is one of the most accessible trails in the park. This short level boardwalk trail winds through a forest that's still recovering from a 1947 glacier generated debris flow, which unleashed a churning mass of mud, rock and vegetation over the area. The boardwalk leads out to an overlook and ends in a viewing area covered in crushed granite, where there are a few benches. There are interpretive plaques about the debris flow along the way, and there's an excellent view of Mount Rainier from the overlook.

Located across the street from the National Park Inn, the Trail of the Shadows is also worth a stop. This hard-packed dirt trail leads through the forest, past beaver lodges and around the site of Longmire's hotel. The trail is wide and level and covered with crushed granite. Interpretive plaques about the eruption of Mount Rainier — some 375,000 years ago — line the trail; and there are benches to sit and rest along the way. The east side of the .7-mile loop is accessible, until you reach the old Longmire cabin. After that there are a few steps down to the bridge, and once you cross the creek

Trail of the Shadows in Mount Rainier National Park

the trail transitions to an uphill and fairly bumpy path. Still, the first part is a nice stroll through the forest, and quite doable for most wheelchair-users and slow walkers.

The Longmire Museum, which is located across the parking lot from the National Park Inn, is a good place to learn about the history of the area. There is level access to the building, and although there is room for a wheelchair inside, it can be tight if it gets crowded. The exhibits focus on the geology, natural history and the first settlements in the area. And for a blast from the past, don't miss the vintage 1937 tour bus outside.

Last but not least, power wheelchair-users might want to check out the Skyline Trail to Lower Myrtle Falls, near the Jackson Visitor Center in Paradise. This trail is rated as "accessible with assistance", and although it's paved, the first part of the trail is a bit steep. Although there's only a 100-foot elevation gain on this half-mile trail, it's all in the same section; however if you can make it past the first steep section, it's fairly level from there on out. This is the most accessible trail in the Paradise area, and it offers a wonderful wildflower view.

The Longmire Museum in Mount Rainier National Park

Don't Miss This

A stop at Christine Falls is a must-do on any Mount Rainier itinerary. Located just east of Longmire, it's on the left side of the road; but if you take time to admire it from the road, you'll completely miss the parking area on the right side. The best view of the falls is from the first pullout, which is located directly across the street from the waterfall, before you reach the main parking area. Unfortunately there are only stairs down to the lower viewing area, but you can still get a nice view of the top part of the 40-foot high waterfall from the 1928 masonry bridge near the pullout.

Insider Tip

For the best access to the Sunrise Visitor Center, it's best to drive behind the restrooms and park near the side entrance, across the street from the picnic area. There is accessible parking in the main lot, but the ramp up to the accessible side entrance from the parking lot is a little steep. Inside, you can get a great view of Mount Rainier from the scope that's trained on the mountain. There is also an accessible picnic table tucked away near the building. It's a nice spot for a quiet lunch as it's not well publicized, and everyone flocks to the more popular picnic area across the street.

Christine Falls in Mount Rainier National Park

Resources

Mount Rainier National Park
(360) 569-2211
www.nps.gov/mora
www.facebook.com/MountRainierNPS
twitter.com/MountRainierNPS

Road Conditions
(360) 569-2211

Rainier Guest Services (NPS Concessionaire)
(360) 569-2275
www.mtrainierguestservices.com
www.facebook.com/RainierLodging
twitter.com/RainierGSLLC
National Park Lodge
Paradise Inn

Barrier-Free Travel; Washington National Parks for Wheelers and Slow Walkers
www.BarrierFreeOlympic.com

Wyoming

String Lake in Grand Teton National Park

Yellowstone National Park

America's first national park spans nearly 3,500 square-miles, the bulk of which occupies the northwestern corner of Wyoming. Known for its geothermal wonders, the park is a filled with gurgling geysers, bubbling mudpots and hidden hot springs. And the good news is, accessible boardwalks and trails skirt many of these geothermal features. But Yellowstone is much more than geysers, as it also boasts dramatic canyons, lush forests, and fertile valleys; which wheelchair-users and slow walkers can enjoy from scenic drives, accessible viewpoints and barrier-free trails throughout the park.

Yellowstone has five entrances. The West Entrance is located just east of the thriving community of West Yellowstone, Montana, along Highway 20. It's the closest entrance to Old Faithful and the Lower Geyser Basin.

The North Entrance is located along Highway 89, near Gardiner, Montana. It offers easy access to the Mammoth Hot Springs area of the park, as well as Norris Geyser Basin.

The Northeast Entrance is located about 3.5 hours southwest of Billings Montana, along Highway 212. Although it's closed during the winter months, this entrance offers proximal access to the Tower-Roosevelt region of the park.

The East Entrance is located 53 miles west of Cody Wyoming, along the Buffalo Bill Cody Scenic Byway. This entrance is close to the Yellowstone Lake, Fishing Bridge and the Canyon Village areas of the park.

The south entrance is about a 1.5-hour drive north of Jackson, Wyoming, along Highway 191. This entrance is close to the West Thumb and Grant Village areas of the park.

Yellowstone National Park is open year-round, but most of the park roads are closed to regular vehicles from early November to mid-April. Once enough snow accumulates — usually by mid-December — the roads are open to concessionaire-operated snowmobiles and snowcoaches for the oversnow travel season. Oversnow travel ends in mid-March, when crews begin plowing the roads, in anticipation of opening them to regular traffic once again in mid-April.

The only park road that's open to regular traffic year-round is the road from the North Entrance at Gardiner. That route travels east through the park towards Tower Junction, exits at the Northeast Entrance and continues on to Cooke City. From Cooke City east, the road — and usually the Northeast Entrance — is closed from late fall to early spring.

It should be noted that weather conditions can change quickly in the spring and fall, and temporary road closures or chain requirements are possible at any time.

There are nine lodges in Yellowstone National Park. Three of them are near Old Faithful, two are in the Yellowstone Lake Area, while the remaining four are located in Grant Village, Tower-Roosevelt, Mammoth and Canyon Junction.

Admission

$35 – seven-day pass
$70 – yearly pass

Old Faithful at Yellowstone National Park

Spend the Night
Old Faithful Snow Lodge & Cabins

1000 Old Faithful Road
Yellowstone National Park, WY 82190
(307) 344-7311
www.yellowstonenationalparklodges.com

Located near the visitor center and the iconic geyser, Old Faithful Snow Lodge is the newest lodging facility in the park. That said, the spacious public areas reflect the ambiance of an old woods lodge, with the use of heavy timbers, wrought iron accents and custom-designed log furniture. Accessible parking is available near the front entrance, with level access to the front doors. Inside, there's barrier-free access throughout the massive lobby, and over to the front desk.

The property has five accessible rooms equipped with roll-in showers, and an accessible cabin with a tub/shower combination.

Room 1009 is located on the first floor, just a short level roll from the lobby. It's furnished with a 25-inch high queen-sized bed and a 25-inch high twin bed, with an access aisle between them, an armoire and a desk with a chair. The bathroom is outfitted with a roll-in shower with grab bars and a hand-held showerhead. The toilet grab bars are located on the back and right walls (as

Old Faithful Snow Lodge

seated), and there's also a roll-under sink right outside the bathroom. A portable shower chair is available for this — or any other — room at the Snow Lodge.

Room 1001 is located down the hall, and it has the same access features and bed configuration as Room 1009. The only difference is that the toilet grab bars are located on the back and left walls (as seated).

Cabin 732 is located a short walk from the main lodge. There's accessible parking in front of the unit, with ramp access up to the front door. The spacious cabin is furnished with two 25-inch high queen-sized beds with wheelchair access between them and on the right side (as you face them), a chest of drawers and a table with two chairs. The bathroom is equipped with a tub/shower combination with grab bars and a hand-held showerhead. The toilet grab bars are located on the back and left walls (as seated), and the bathroom has a roll-under sink. A portable shower chair is also available.

There's barrier-free access to all the public areas in the main lodge building, including the gift shop, Geyser Grill, the Obsidian Dining Room and the Firehole Lounge. And since this property is close to Old Faithful, guests can explore the area at a leisurely place, and come back to the lodge for a break if they get tired.

Old Faithful Snow Lodge is open from late April to mid-October for all guests, and from mid-December to early March for oversnow traffic only.

Cabin 732 at Old Faithful Snow Lodge

Old Faithful Inn

1 Grand Loop Road
Yellowstone National Park, WY 82190
(307) 344-7311
www.yellowstonenationalparklodges.com

Crafted from local logs and stone, the earliest section of this historic property dates back to 1903. The rustic lobby features a 76-foot tall ceiling, with balcony railings crafted from gnarled logs. Top it off with a centerpiece roughstone fireplace, and you can see why this building is a favorite of many park visitors. Even if you don't stay here, it's definitely worth a visit.

There's level access to the front lobby, with plenty of room to maneuver a wheelchair inside. Old Faithful Inn offers six accessible rooms. Room 2 is located a short distance from the front lobby in the "old house" section of the property. It's furnished with a 25-inch high queen-sized bed with wheelchair access on the right side (as you face it). Room 6, which is located on the other side of a shared bathroom, is also furnished with a 25-inch high queen-sized bed, but it has wheelchair access on the left side (as you face it).

The accessible bathroom is only shared by these two rooms, and it requires key access from the hallway. There's a full five-foot turning radius in this

Lobby at the Old Faithful Inn

Room 2 in "the old house" at the Old Faithful Inn

renovated historic space, which still features a steam radiator and black-and-white chicken wire tile floors. It's equipped with a roll-in shower with grab bars and a portable shower bench. The toilet grab bars are located on the back and right walls (as seated), and there's also a roll-under sink in the bathroom.

If you'd prefer more modern accommodations, Room 2032 is located in the newest (1927) section of the property. It features good pathway access and is furnished with a 26-inch high queen-sized bed with wheelchair access on

Bathroom shared by rooms 2 and 6 in "the old house" at the Old Faithful Inn

Room 2032 at the Old Faithful Inn

both sides, a table with two chairs and a chest of drawers. The bathroom has a tub/shower combination with grab bars and a hand-held showerhead. The toilet grab bars are located on the back and left walls (as seated), and there's a roll-under sink right outside the bathroom door. A portable shower chair is available for this — or any — room at the inn.

Room 2050, which is located down the hall, is furnished with a 26-inch high queen-sized bed with wheelchair access on the left side (as you face it), a table with two chairs, and a chest of drawers. The bathroom has the same

Bathroom in room 2032 at the Old Faithful Inn

Room 2050 at the Old Faithful Inn

access features as room 2032, except that the toilet grab bars are located on the back and right walls (as seated). Both rooms are incredibly spacious by today's standards, and downright decadent 90 years ago.

There's barrier-free access to all the public areas of the inn as well, including the gift shop, the Bear Paw Deli, the Bear Pit Lounge and the extremely popular Old Faithful Inn Dining Room. There is also elevator access to the 1927 section of the building.

Old Faithful Inn is open from early May to early October.

Old Faithful Lodge Cabins

1000 Old Faithful Village
Yellowstone National Park, WY 82190
(307) 344-7311
www.yellowstonenationalparklodges.com

Designed by Gilbert Stanley Underwood, Old Faithful Lodge bears a striking resemblance to the Ahwahnee in Yosemite National Park. There's barrier-free access to the massive lobby which features floor-to-ceiling windows that offer a commanding view of Old Faithful. There's good pathway access through the lobby of this 1923 property, and barrier-free access over to the front desk. The lodge offers eight accessible cabins, all of which have roll-in showers.

Cabin 161 is located a short walk from the main lodge, and it has accessible parking in front, with level access over to the front door. Access features include good pathway access, wide doorways and a lowered closet rod. The cabin is furnished with two 24-inch high queen-sized beds with wheelchair access on all sides, and a desk with a chair. The bathroom is equipped with a roll-in shower with grab bars and a hand-held showerhead. The toilet grab bars are located on the back and right walls (as seated), and the bathroom also has a roll-under sink and a portable shower chair.

Cabin 161 at Old Faithful Lodge Cabins

Bedroom in cabin 161 at Old Faithful Lodge Cabins

Bathroom in cabin 161 at Old Faithful Lodge Cabins

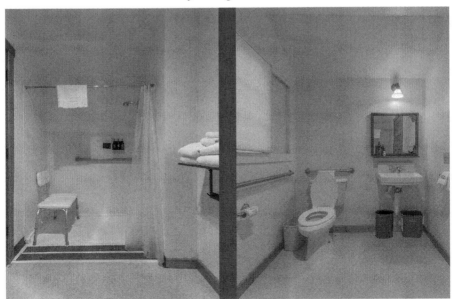

There's good wheelchair access to all of the public areas in the main lodge building, including the gift shop, Old Faithful Lodge Cafeteria, the Bakery & Snack Shop, and the public restrooms. And it's a great place to watch the geyser erupt, when the weather is bad.

This property is open from mid-May to early October.

Lake Yellowstone Hotel & Cabins

Lake Village
Yellowstone National Park, WY 82190
(307) 344-7311
www.yellowstonenationalparklodges.com

This lakeshore property, which dates back to 1891, underwent a massive renovation in 2014. Today the colonial revival building that houses the main hotel, and the historic cabins on the far side of the parking lot, together offer a number of accessible lodging options for wheelchair-users and slow walkers. And with the Grand Canyon of the Yellowstone River just a short drive away, Lake Yellowstone Hotel makes a convenient home base for folks who want to explore the rugged scenery in the canyon area by day, and return to a placid lake view each evening.

Accessible parking is available in the large parking lot behind the hotel,

Lake Yellowstone Hotel

Room 226 at the Lake Yellowstone Hotel

with level access over to the entrance. Inside there's good wheelchair access throughout the lobby, and a barrier-free pathway over to the registration desk. This property has 18 accessible rooms and cabins, 7 of which have roll-in showers.

There's elevator access up to room 226, which is furnished with two 25-inch high queen-sized beds with wheelchair access on all sides. Other furnishings include a table with two chairs, a bedside table and an armoire. There's good pathway access and wide doorways throughout the whole room. The spacious bathroom

Bathroom in room 226 at the Lake Yellowstone Hotel

Bathroom in room 126 at the Lake Yellowstone Hotel

is equipped with a tub/shower combination with grab bars, a hand-held showerhead and a portable shower chair. Toilet grab bars located on the back and right walls (as seated), and there's also a roll-under sink in the bathroom.

Room 126, which is located on the first floor, has the same bed configuration and basic access features as room 226. The bathroom has a roll-in shower, with grab bars, a hand-held showerhead and a portable shower bench. The toilet has grab bars on the back and right walls (as seated), and the spacious room also has a roll-under sink. The access

Room 202 at the Lake Yellowstone Hotel

Bathroom in room 202 at the Lake Yellowstone Hotel

features are nicely incorporated into the historic design of the room, and they even remembered to lower the soap dish in the shower.

Room 202 is a spacious corner room which features wide doorways, a lowered peephole and excellent pathway access. It's furnished with a 25-inch high king-sized bed with wheelchair access on both sides, two chairs, an armoire and two bedside tables. The bathroom, which features a full five-foot turning radius, is equipped with a tub/shower combination with grab bars, a hand-held showerhead and a portable shower bench. Other bathroom access features include toilet grab bars on the back and left walls (as seated), and a roll-under sink.

Room 446 is a spacious accessible suite, which features wide doorways and good pathway access. The living area is furnished with a 16-inch high sleeper sofa, a chair, and a coffee table. It also includes a wet bar with a refrigerator. The separate bedroom includes a 25-inch high king-sized bed with wheelchair access on both sides, a table with two chairs, a desk with a chair and two bedside tables. Because of the separate sleeping facilities, this room is a good choice for someone traveling with an attendant.

The spacious bathroom includes a roll-in shower with grab bars, a hand-held showerhead and a portable shower bench; as well as a separate tub with grab bars. The toilet grab bars are located on the back and right walls (as seated), and the bathroom also includes a roll-under sink.

Suite 446 at the Lake Yellowstone Hotel

Bedroom in suite 446 at the Lake Yellowstone Hotel

Sink and toilet in suite 446 at the Lake Yellowstone Hotel

Bathtub and shower in suite 446 at the Lake Yellowstone Hotel

Cabin 635 at the Lake Yellowstone Hotel

Cabin 635 is located a short level walk from the main hotel building. There's accessible parking in front of the unit, with curb-cut access up to a level pathway to the front door. It's furnished with a 25-inch high double bed with wheelchair access on both sides. The bathroom is equipped with a

Bedroom in cabin 635 at the Lake Yellowstone Hotel

Bathroom in cabin 635 at the Lake Yellowstone Hotel

roll-in shower with grab bars, a hand-held showerhead and a fold-down shower bench. The toilet grab bars are located on the back and right walls (as seated), and there's also a roll-under sink located in the bedroom.

Cabin 636, which is located next door, has the same access features, except that the toilet grab bars are located on the back and left walls (as seated).

There's good wheelchair access to all the public areas of the hotel, including the gift shop, the Lake Hotel Deli, the Lake Hotel Lounge, and the incredibly scenic Lake Hotel Dining Room. The spacious lobby features comfortable seating and also offers a nice view of the lake. Additionally there's level access to the large porch, where you can get an equally enticing view.

Lake Lodge Cabins

Old Faithful Bypass Road
Yellowstone National Park, WY 82190
(307) 344-7311
www.yellowstonenationalparklodges.com

Located down the road from the Lake Yellowstone Hotel, Lake Lodge offers comfortable accommodations in historic cabins. The main lodge building, which is the focal point of the property, is constructed of logs and exudes a definite mountain ambiance. The cabins are scattered around the main building, and the inventory includes 10 accessible units, all of which have roll-in showers.

Cabin B4 features accessible parking on the side with ramp access up to the front porch. Access features include wide doorways, good pathway access, and a lowered clothing rod. The cabin is furnished with a 25-inch high twin bed (with a trundle), and a 25-inch high queen-sized bed, with an access aisle between them. The bathroom is equipped with a roll-in shower with grab bars, a hand-held showerhead and a fold-down shower bench. The toilet grab bars are located on the back and left walls (as seated), and there is a roll-under sink in the bedroom. All in in it's a very comfortable and accessible cabin.

Cabin B4 at Lake Lodge Cabins

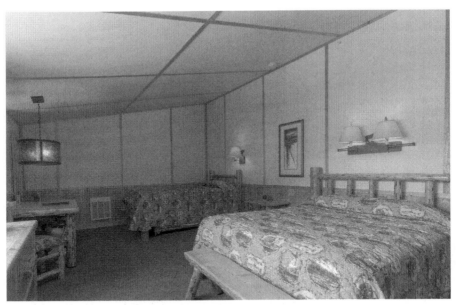

Bedroom in cabin B4 at Lake Lodge Cabins

There's good access to the main lodge as well, with a level drop-off area in front, and curb-cut-access up to the ramped entry. Inside, there's plenty of room to maneuver a wheelchair around the rustic lobby, with barrier-free access over to the registration desk and gift shop, and ramp access up to the Lake Lodge Cafeteria. It's the perfect place to stay if you really want to get a feel for old Yellowstone, yet still have the creature comforts – and access — of today.

Lake Lodge is open from early June to late September.

Bathroom in cabin B4 at Lake Lodge Cabins

Grant Village Lodge

West Thumb Geyser Basin Trail
Yellowstone National Park, WY 82190
(307) 344-7311
www.yellowstonenationalparklodges.com

Tucked away in a lodgepole pine forest, just a few miles from the thermal features at West Thumb, Grant Village Lodge was named after the president who established Yellowstone as the nation's first national park in 1872. The spacious property features six two-story lodges, and because of the strategic placement of the buildings, you never really feel like you're at a large hotel. That said, this cozy mountain property certainly has all the comforts of home. Grant Village Lodge has 12 accessible rooms, all of which have roll-in showers.

Accessible parking is located in front of the registration building, with level access to the front door. Inside there's good pathway access to the lobby, gift shop and registration desk. Room 3102 is located a short walk or drive away in the Coyote Lodge. Accessible parking is located near the front door of the lodge building, and there's a level sidewalk over to the entrance, and barrier-free access to the room.

This ground floor room features wide doorways, good pathway access, and

Bedroom in room 3102 at Grant Village Lodge

Bathroom in room 3102 at Grant Village Lodge

lowered drapery wands. It's furnished with a 26-inch high queen-sized bed with wheelchair access on both sides, two bedside tables, a table with two chairs and a refrigerator. The spacious bathroom is equipped with a roll-in shower with grab bars, a hand-held showerhead and a fold-down shower seat. Other access features include toilet grab bars on the back and left walls (as seated), and a roll-under sink.

This nicely accessible property is one of the park's best kept secrets, largely because some of the more famous properties get the lion's share of the press. Still it's a great pick for a very comfortable — and accessible — Yellowstone stay.

Grant Village Lodge is open from mid-May to early October.

Canyon Lodge & Cabins

3 Canyon Loop Drive
North Rim Drive
Yellowstone National Park, WY 82190
(307) 344-7311
www.yellowstonenationalparklodges.com

The largest property in the park, Canyon Lodge, is located on the east side, near the Grand Canyon of the Yellowstone River. It features 590 rooms scattered in lodge buildings and cabins throughout a large wooded parcel.

Room 1136 at Canyon Lodge & Cabins

That said, the distance between them isn't a problem, as accessible shuttle service is available from all the lodge buildings to the dining facilities, retail outlets and the visitor center in nearby Canyon Village. This property underwent a massive renovation project in 2017, which included a number

Bathroom in room 1136 at Canyon Lodge & Cabins

of access upgrades. Today, Canyon Lodge has 30 accessible lodge rooms and five accessible western cabins.

Washburn Lodge serves as the reception center for the property. There's plenty of accessible parking in front and level access to the front door. Inside there's barrier-free access to the registration desk, a small sitting area and accessible restrooms. There's also a large drop-off area in front of the building.

Room 1136 is located in Washburn Lodge, just a short walk from the front desk. Access features include a wide doorway with a lowered peephole, a lowered closet rod, and ample pathway access to maneuver a wheelchair.

This superior lodge room is furnished with two 26-inch high queen-sized beds with an access aisle between them, a table and two chairs, and a refrigerator. There's also a roll-under sink in the bedroom. The bathroom is equipped with a tub/shower combination with grab bars and a hand-held showerhead. The toilet grab bars are located on the back and right walls (as seated), and the bathroom also has a portable shower chair.

Room 4305 is an accessible standard lodge room, which has the same basic access features as room 1136. It's furnished with a 26-inch high

Room 4305 at Canyon Lodge & Cabins

Bathroom in room 4305 at Canyon Lodge & Cabins

queen-sized bed with wheelchair access on both sides, and a table with two chairs. The bathroom includes a roll-in shower with grab bars, a hand-held showerhead and a portable shower bench. The toilet grab bars are on the back and left walls (as seated), and a roll-under sink is located in the bedroom.

Room 5210 at Canyon Lodge & Cabins

Bathroom in room 5210 at Canyon Lodge & Cabins

Room 5210 is an accessible premium lodge room. It's furnished with a 26-inch high queen-sized bed and a 26-inch high twin bed with an access aisle between them. There are also two chairs in the bedroom area. The bathroom has a roll-in shower with grab bars, a hand-held showerhead and a portable shower bench. Other bathroom access features include toilet grab bars on the back and right walls (as seated), and a roll-under sink.

Living space in room 1213 at Canyon Lodge & Cabins

Queen-sized bed in room 1213 at Canyon Lodge & Cabins

Room 1213 is an accessible two-bedroom suite, which features wide doors, a lowered clothing rod and barrier-free access throughout the unit. The living area includes a table and two chairs, a 14-inch high sleeper sofa, and a wet bar with a refrigerator. One bedroom is furnished with a 26-inch high queen-sized bed, with wheelchair access

King-sized bed in room 1213 at Canyon Lodge & Cabins

Bathroom in room 1213 at Canyon Lodge & Cabins

on both sides, and a desk with a chair. There's also level access out to a large balcony from this this bedroom. The other bedroom is furnished with a 26-inch high king-sized bed with wheelchair access on both sides, and an easy chair.

The bathroom is equipped with a tub/shower combination with grab bars, a hand-held showerhead and a portable shower chair. The toilet grab bars are located on the back and left walls (as seated), and the accessible roll-under sink is located right outside the bathroom. There are two of these second-floor suites in each lodge building. They all have elevator access, and 50% of these spacious rooms are wheelchair-accessible.

Cabin 32, which is located a short drive from Washburn Lodge, features accessible parking in front with level access to the front door. It's furnished with a 24-inch high twin bed (with a trundle), and a 26-inch high open-framed queen-sized bed, with an access aisle between them. It also has a table with two chairs next to two large windows that offer a good view of the surrounding lodgepole pine forest.

The bathroom is equipped with a roll-in shower with a grab bars, a hand-held showerhead and a fold-down shower bench. The toilet grab bars are located on the back and left walls (as seated) and there's a roll-under sink just outside the bathroom.

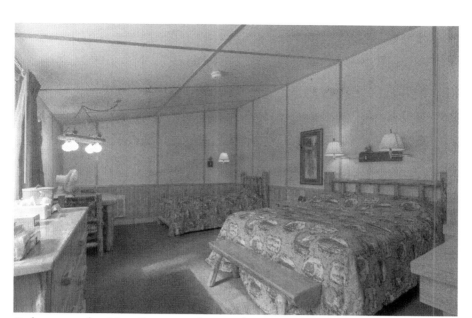

Bedroom in cabin 32 at Canyon Lodge & Cabins

Truly, Canyon Lodge has a room to suit just about every taste and budget. There's also barrier-free access to all the public areas at this property; and all the lodge buildings, except Cascade, have elevators. A portable shower chair is also available for any room upon request.

Canyon Lodge is open from early June to early October.

Bathroom in cabin 32 at Canyon Lodge & Cabins

Roosevelt Lodge Cabins

Tower-Roosevelt Junction
Yellowstone National Park, WY 82190
(307) 344-7311
www.yellowstonenationalparklodges.com

Located near Tower Junction, these historic cabins were built in 1920, close to a campsite used by the namesake president. Today some access modifications have been added to the property; however it's still quite rustic. That's said, it's a favorite for families, and for anyone who wants to get that "old west" experience. As an added bonus, it's not unusual to see bison grazing in the area.

Accessible parking is located in front of the main lodge, with ramped access on the left to the large front porch lined with rocking chairs. There's level access to the lobby, that's accented with wood floors, log beams and western chandeliers; and barrier-free access over to the registration desk, bar, gift shop and the Roosevelt Lodge Dining Room. Accessible restrooms are located behind the registration desk.

Accessible cabin 86 is located a short walk — or drive — away. The .15 mile level dirt road to the cabin has a few rocks here and there; but they are easy to dodge if you can manage the distance. There's no striped parking next to

Main lodge at Roosevelt Lodge Cabins

Cabin 86 at Roosevelt Lodge Cabins

the rustic cabin, but there is a large level spot next to it, with plenty of room to park an accessible van.

Access features in the cabin include ramp access, wide doorways, barrier-free pathways and wood floors for easy rolling. It's furnished with a 25-inch high double bed with wheelchair access on both sides, a night table, and a desk with a chair. It also includes a heater, a fan, and plenty of electrical outlets.

There's barrier-free access to the bathroom, which boasts a full five-foot turning radius. It's equipped with a roll-in shower with grab bars, a hand-held showerhead and a portable shower seat. The toilet grab bars are located on the back and left walls (as seated), and the bathroom also has a roll-under sink with a lowered mirror. They thought of everything in this cabin, including a lowered robe hook. And they even remembered some special homey touches, like a bear-shaped bar of soap.

Cabin 90, which is located across from cabin 86, also has the same access features.

Either cabin is a good choice for wheelchair-users or slow walkers who want something a little different from a standard hotel room. And although you won't find a dedicated concierge, spa services or other luxury perks there, the cabins are certainly cozy, comfortable and accessible.

Bedroom in cabin 86 at Roosevelt Lodge Cabins

It should be noted that this property is the earliest one in the park to close, so plan ahead. The Roosevelt Lodge Cabins are open from early June to early September.

Bathroom in cabin 86 at Roosevelt Lodge Cabins

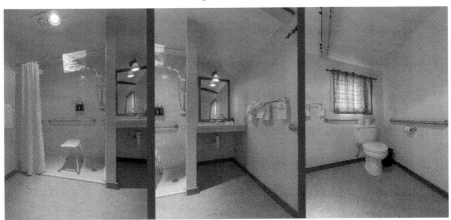

Mammoth Hot Springs Hotel & Cabins

Grand Loop Road
Yellowstone National Park, WY 82190
(307) 344-7311
www.yellowstonenationalparklodges.com

Built in 1936, this property incorporated a wing of rooms from the former National Hotel into the construction plans. Named for the nearby hot springs, this hotel offers two accessible rooms in the historic wing, and four accessible cabins a short walk from the main lobby — all of which have roll-in showers. As an added bonus, this area is a favorite spot for the resident elk, who can often be found grazing near Fort Yellowstone or even behind the main hotel building.

Accessible parking is located behind the main lodge, with a paved level pathway around to the front door. There's barrier-free access to the main building, and plenty of room to maneuver a wheelchair through the large lobby, and over to the registration desk.

Room 101, which is located just off the lobby, features wide doorways, good pathway access and a lowered clothing rod. It's furnished with a 26-inch high queen-sized bed with wheelchair-access on both sides, a bedside table, a chest of drawers and a chair. The bathroom, which is equally spacious, is equipped with a roll-in shower with grab bars, a hand-held showerhead and a fold-down shower bench. Other access features include toilet grab bars on the back and left walls (as seated), and a roll-under sink.

Mammoth Hot Springs Hotel and Cabins

Room 101 at Mammoth Hot Springs Hotel and Cabins

Room 111, which is located down the hall, has the same access features as room 101.

Cabin B 20, which is located behind the main lodge building, features level parking next to the cabin, with ramp access to the front porch. Inside there's plenty of room to maneuver a wheelchair around the 23-inch high queen-sized bed. Other furnishings include a desk with a chair, and two bedside tables. The small closet also has a lowered clothing rod. The bathroom is

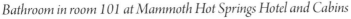

Bathroom in room 101 at Mammoth Hot Springs Hotel and Cabins

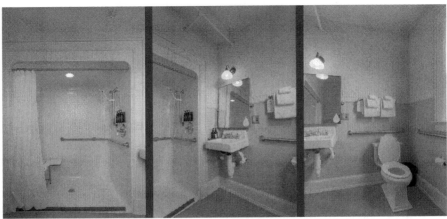

Cabin B 20 at Mammoth Hot Springs Hotel and Cabins

outfitted with a roll-in shower with grab bars, a hand-held showerhead and a fold-down shower bench. The toilet grab bars are located on the back and right walls (as seated), and the bathroom is also equipped with a roll-under sink and a portable shower chair.

Bedroom in cabin B 20 at Mammoth Hot Springs Hotel and Cabins

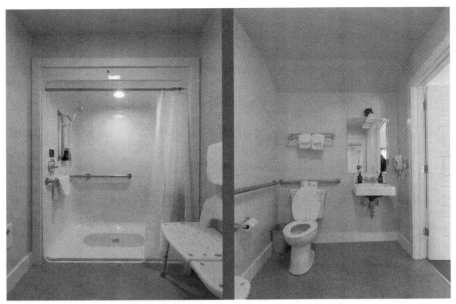

Bathroom in cabin B 20 at Mammoth Hot Springs Hotel and Cabins

Cabin B 11 has the same access features as cabin B 20. Cabin B 10 is a mirror image of Cabin B 20, and it has the toilet grab bars on the back and left walls (as seated). A portable shower chair is also available for any room — or cabin — upon request.

There's good access to all of the public areas off the main lobby, including the gift shop, and the accessible restrooms. Picture windows offer a nice view of the surrounding landscape, and wood floors make for easy rolling around the public spaces. And although renovations have been made over the years, this property still retains the ambiance of the original 1930s hotel. It's a great place to relax, and it makes a nice home base for exploring the geothermal features at the north end of the park.

This property is open from late April to early October, and from mid-December to early March.

Access Overview

The good news about Yellowstone is, even though it's a large park with a diverse and healthy wildlife population, there are accessible trails, attractions and activities in nearly every area. That said, sometimes the wildlife congregates on the park roads — locally known as bison jams — so allow plenty of extra time for your travels. Elevation can also be an issue in some areas of the park, like 8,878-foot Dunraven Pass; however many of the well touristed sites have elevations well below that. Reese Creek, with an elevation of 5,282 feet, is the lowest point in the park.

There are no restrictions on private vehicles on the park roads, but if you'd like to leave the driving to someone else, the Xanterra Travel Collection offers a number of accessible bus tours. The tours, which range from a 1.5-hour introduction to the park, to a full-day adventure, are conducted in 12-passenger accessible buses. Accessible snowcoach tours and transfers are also available in the oversnow travel season. All accessible tours must be booked at least 48 hours in advance.

The Xanterra Travel Collection also offers accessible Yellowstone Lake cruises from mid-June to early September. The *Lake Queen* features accessible boarding at the Bridge Bay Marina, and has two sets of tie-downs aboard. This one-hour cruise circles Stevenson Island, before it follows the

Bison jam in Yellowstone National Park

shoreline on the lookout for native wildlife. Along the way, passengers are treated to a narrative about the history of the area, and some of the colorful characters who once called this place home. Advance reservations are highly recommended for this popular cruise.

The most popular attraction in the park is the iconic Old Faithful Geyser. Several level paved pathways lead from the visitor center to a boardwalk which circles the geyser. Benches line the boardwalk, and there's plenty of room for wheelchairs and scooters next to them; however to be honest, you don't need a front row seat for the show, as you can see the eruption from just about anywhere along the boardwalk. And if you want to save your energy or escape the weather, you can also view the event from the visitor center.

The multiuse trail to Morning Glory Pool is also a good choice for some wheelchair-users and slow walkers. The accessible 1.4-mile trail begins across from the gas station, on the far side of Old Faithful Inn. The trail travels through the forest and past Castle Geyser, Grotto Geyser and Riverside Geyser; before it reaches Fan, Mortar and Spiteful Geysers and Morning Glory Pool at the end of the line. It's a pleasant walk, and Morning Glory Pool — which resembles the namesake flower — is definitely one of the more unusual thermal features in the park.

Other accessible geothermal areas near Old Faithful include Black Sand Basin, Biscuit Basin and Midway Geyser Basin. Named for the sand derived

Castle Geyser on the multiuse trail to Morning Glory Pool

from the black volcanic glass in this area, Black Sand Basin features some of the most colorful hot springs in the park. A .6-mile boardwalk leads out around the geysers, but if you can't manage the walk, there are several striking features near the parking area. Biscuit Basin, which gets its name from the unusual biscuit-like formations that once surrounded Sapphire Pool, features an .8 mile accessible boardwalk trail. And Midway Geyser Basin has a mile-long accessible boardwalk, which circles Excelsior Geyser, Turquoise Pool, Opal Pool and Grand Prismatic Spring — the largest hot spring in the park.

Firehole Lake Drive, which is also located along the road to Old Faithful, features a scenic drive past several geysers, with numerous accessible pullouts and trails along the way. As an added bonus, it's not unusual to spot bison along the first section of the drive; and there's nothing quit like hearing their eerie grunts and groans from the boardwalks around the nearby geysers. Additionally, this route is pleasantly devoid of tour buses, as larger vehicles are prohibited on Firehole Lake Drive.

Another accessible geothermal area is located a short drive southeast of Old Faithful in West Thumb Geyser Basin. A half-mile boardwalk trail passes by the thumb paint pots and offers a good view of the central basin with the mountains in the background. And if you'd like to linger, there are numerous benches to take a break and enjoy the view.

The Canyon area of the park offers a number of scenic drives with accessible

Trail at Black Sand Basin

trails and viewpoints along the way. North Rim Drive is a one-way route that's located just south of Canyon Village, and offers panoramic views of the Grand Canyon of the Yellowstone River. South Rim Drive is a larger two-way road, that features more expansive canyon views. And don't forget to stop at the Brink of the Upper Falls, which is located midway between North Rim Drive, and South Rim Drive. The trail down to the left has steps and a steep grade; however if you bear right and continue along the South Rim Trail you'll be treated to an impressive view of the falls.

Finally, up in the north section of the park, be sure to visit Upper Terrace Drive, which begins about two miles south of Albright Visitor Center. Canary Spring and Orange Spring Mound are worth a stop along this scenic route, as they both have accessible boardwalk trails. It's important to note that the accessible boardwalk trail to Canary Spring begins directly across from the accessible parking area — don't take the inaccessible trail to the right.

Located down the street from the Mammoth Gas Station, Lower Terraces also offers a wheelchair-accessible boardwalk trail. Best bet is to park in one of the accessible parking spaces near Liberty Cap, for level access to the boardwalk. Although there's a slight uphill grade to the trail, there are level spots to stop on the .1-mile boardwalk out to Palette Spring. This colorful spring gets its name from the watercolor effect that the orange and brown waters cause as they flow down the steep ridge. It's an extremely photogenic site.

Orange Spring Mound on Upper Terrace Drive

Don't Miss This

Although the geysers are a big draw in Yellowstone, the Museum of the National Park Ranger is definitely worth a visit. As the retired ranger who staffed the museum put it, "This museum is about the people in the parks, not the animals or the geology." Housed in a historic building that was once an army barracks, and then a ranger station, the Museum of the National Park Ranger is located north of Norris Geyser Basin, just down the road from Norris Campground.

There's a paved level path to the museum, which houses exhibits that describe ranger duties in the different parks, and include displays of ranger equipment, uniforms and emergency supplies. There's also a mock-up of a back country ranger cabin, and a small display that depicts what the museum building looked like when it served as an army barracks. Add in a nice collection of historic photos, and a scenic river view from the back porch, and you have a multitude of reasons to visit this museum.

Insider Tip

Forces of the Northern Range — a secluded boardwalk tucked away along the road between Tower Junction and Mammoth Hot Springs — is often

Inside the Museum of the National Park Ranger

overlooked by visitors. Don't make that mistake. It's easy to miss, as it's only marked by a small brown "self-guided trail" roadside sign.

The half-mile accessible boardwalk winds through the sagebrush and shrub-lined landscape and features scenic views of Yellowstone's Northern Range in the distance. Interpretive plaques that detail the flora, fauna and geology of the area are dotted along the boardwalk, and several short spurs lead out to secluded areas that are lined with benches. And even though it's a short trail, because of the spurs and vegetation you never feel crowded. It's a very well designed trail, with magnificent views of the surrounding landscape; and truly one of Yellowstone's hidden gems.

Resources

Yellowstone National Park
(307) 344-7381
www.nps.gov/yell
www.facebook.com/YellowstoneNPS
twitter.com/YellowstoneNPS

Road Conditions (recorded)
(307) 344-2117

Xanterra Travel Collection (NPS Concessionaire)
(307) 344-7311
www.yellowstonenationalparklodges.com
https://twitter.com/YNPLodges
Old Faithful Snow Lodge & Cabins
Old Faithful Inn
Old Faithful Lodge Cabins
Lake Yellowstone Hotel & Cabins
Lake Lodge Cabins
Grant Village Lodge
Canyon Lodge & Cabins
Roosevelt Lodge Cabins
Mammoth Hot Springs Hotel & Cabins

Barrier-Free Travel; Glacier, Yellowstone and Grand Teton National Parks for Wheelers and Slow Walkers
www.barrierfreeyellowstone.com

Grand Teton National Park

L ocated south of the John D. Rockefeller, Jr. Memorial Parkway and north of Jackson, Wyoming, Grand Teton National Park encompasses over 310,000 acres filled with glacial lakes and bordered by the magnificent Teton Range. But don't let the rugged landscape fool you, as recent access improvements at Jenny Lake, coupled with the extension of the accessible multiuse trail, continue to make Grand Teton National Park an attractive option for wheelchair-users and slow walkers. And since the park is just a short drive from Yellowstone, it's easy to plan an accessible road trip that includes both parks.

There are four entrances to Grand Teton National Park.

The North Entrance is located along Highway 89-191-287, on the south border of the John D. Rockefeller, Jr. Memorial Parkway.

The Moran Entrance is located on the east side of the park. It's 60 miles northwest of Dubois, Wyoming, along Highway 27-287, a scenic route that's also known as the Togwotee Trail.

The Granite Canyon Entrance is located on Moose-Wilson Road in the southwest section of the park, just east of Teton Village.

The Moose Entrance is located along Highway 26-89-191, 13 miles north of Jackson, Wyoming.

Grand Teton National Park is open year-round, but some of the park roads are closed during the winter season. The main park road (Teton Park Road) is closed from Taggart Lake Trailhead to Signal Mountain Lodge from November 1 through April 30. Signal Mountain Summit Road and a section of Moose-Wilson Road (from the Granite Canyon Trailhead to the Death Canyon Trailhead) are closed to vehicle traffic from November 1 until they can be cleared of snow, which is usually some time in mid-May. Additionally, some of the smaller park roads, such as Antelope Flats, are closed in the winter, and reopened when conditions permit. It should be noted that weather conditions can change quickly in the spring and fall, and temporary road closures are possible at any time.

There are four lodges with accessible rooms or cabins in Grand Teton National Park.

Admission

$35 – seven-day pass
$70 – yearly pass

Spend the Night

Jenny Lake Lodge

Jenny Lake Road
Moose, WY 83012
(307) 543-3100
www.gtlc.com

Located near the foot of the Tetons on the east shore of scenic Jenny Lake, this historic resort dates back to the 1920s, when a dude ranch with two rental cabins occupied the site. Over the years, there have been a bevy of upgrades and improvements to the property, yet the 37 log cabins that dot the forest-covered grounds at Jenny Lake Lodge still retain their historic ambiance. And historic doesn't necessarily means bare-bones either, as there's certainly no shortage of creature comforts at this AAA four-diamond resort.

Jenny Lake Lodge at Grand Teton National Park

Accessible parking is located outside of the main lodge, with curb-cut access up to a level pathway to the front entrance. A veritable stable of rocking chairs lines the front porch, and inside a large fireplace dominates the massive lobby. The registration desk is located next to the dining room, just steps from the accessible front entrance. Jenny Lake Lodge has two accessible cabins.

One accessible duplex cabin — Tansy — is located a .15-mile walk from the main lodge, on a pleasant paved pathway through the forest. Parking is also available in back of the cabin, in a wide, level, paved space, with a barrier-free path over to the front door.

Access features inside the cabin — which was constructed in the 1990s — include wide doorways, good pathway access, wood floors for easy rolling, and a lowered closet space. The bedroom is furnished with a 25-inch high king-sized bed with wheelchair access on both sides, two easy chairs and a small desk with a chair. It also includes a wet bar with a sink, and a small refrigerator.

The bathroom features a full five-foot turning radius, and is equipped with a tub/shower combination with grab bars, and a small ledge opposite the faucet. A portable shower chair is also available upon request. Other bathroom access features include toilet grab bars on the back and left walls (as seated) and a roll-under sink.

Tansy cabin at Jenny Lake Lodge

Bedroom in the Tansy cabin at Jenny Lake Lodge

All in all, it's a very roomy and luxurious cabin. Add in an in-room telephone and free Wi-Fi, and you'll also be able to stay connected during your stay.

There's good access to all the public areas at Jenny Lake Lodge, including the accessible restrooms, and gift shop. The Jenny Lake Lodge Dining Room, which features barrier-free access, serves traditional favorites in the morning, a selection of burgers, sandwiches, soups, salads and entrees for lunch, and offers an elegant five-course prix-fixe menu in the evening.

Bathroom in the Tansy cabin at Jenny Lake Lodge

Reservations are required for dinner, and recommended for lunch, especially during the busy summer season.

Jenny Lake Lodge is open from early June to early October.

Jackson Lake Lodge

101 Jackson Lake Lodge Road
Moran, WY 83013
(307) 543-3100
www.gtlc.com

Located near the eastern shore of the park's largest lake, Jackson Lake Lodge offers a panoramic view of the Teton Range with the namesake lake in the foreground. This 385-room property boasts a decidedly 1950s architectural style, yet offers all the creature comforts — including free Wi-Fi — of the present decade. And with the cottages and lodges spaced throughout the large parcel, this property manages to maintain a fairly relaxed ambiance.

Accessible parking is located in front of the main lodge, with level access over to the lower lobby. Inside, there's plenty of room to maneuver a wheelchair, with barrier-free access over to the lowered registration desk. An accessible drop-off area is also located in front of the property, and automatic doors lead into the main building. Jackson Lake Lodge offers 20 accessible rooms, in a variety of bed configurations, room types and access categories.

Main lobby at Jackson Lake Lodge

Room 18 at Jackson Lake Lodge

Room 18 is located in the main lodge, and is classified as a Type 1 accessible room. Access features include wide doorways, lowered clothing hooks, lever handles and good pathway access. It's furnished with two 27-inch high queen-sized beds with wheelchair access between them, two easy chairs, a chest of drawers and a wet bar with a refrigerator. It also has a to-die-for mountain view.

The bathroom is equipped with a tub/shower combination with grab bars, a sink with knee space, and a toilet with grab bars on the back and right walls (as seated). Type 1 accessible rooms do not have hand-held showerheads, and typically these rooms are a good choice for slow walkers and part-time wheelchair-users.

Bathroom in room 18 at Jackson Lake Lodge

320

Room 302 at Jackson Lake Lodge

Room 302, which is located a short drive from the main lodge, is a classic cottage with Type 1 accessibility features. Accessible parking is located near the unit, with level access over to the front door. Access feature include wide doorways, good pathway access and a lowered clothing rod. The room

Bedroom in room 302 at Jackson Lake Lodge

is furnished with two 27-inch high queen-sized beds with wheelchair access in the center, a chair, and a wet bar with a refrigerator. The bathroom is the same as the one in room 18.

The Moose Pond Suite (room 906) also has Type 1 accessibility features. Accessible parking is located near this ground-floor room, with barrier-free access over to the front door. Access features include wide doorways, good pathway access and a lowered clothing rod.

The room is furnished with a 27-inch high king-sized bed with wheelchair access on both sides, a table with two chairs, two night tables and a chest of drawers. This spacious room also includes a wet bar and a refrigerator.

There's level access to the adjacent patio through a wide door, and although a chair needs to be moved to access the door, there's plenty of room to relocate it in the spacious suite. Outside, there's ample room for a wheelchair, on the patio that's furnished with two chairs. And if the weather is a bit nippy, you can also enjoy the beautiful mountain view through the picture window from inside the comfy heated room.

The roomy bathroom is furnished with a tub/shower combination with grab bars, and it includes a small ledge seat opposite the shower controls. A sink with knee clearance, and a toilet with grab bars on the back and right walls (as seated), are also included in the bathroom.

Moose Pond Suite at Jackson Lake Lodge

Wet bar in the Moose Pond Suite at Jackson Lake Lodge

Room 401 is a classic cottage, with Type 2 access features. Accessible parking is located near the unit, with level access up to the front door. The room features wide doorways and good pathway access, and is furnished with two 27-inch high queen-sized beds with an access aisle in the middle.

Bathroom in the Moose Pond Suite at Jackson Lake Lodge

Other furnishings include a chair, and a wet bar with a refrigerator.

The bathroom is equipped with a tub/shower combination with grab bars and a hand-held showerhead. Other bathroom access features include a roll-under sink and a toilet with grab bars on the back and left walls (as seated).

Room 202 is also a classic cottage, but it is equipped with Type 3 accessibility features. All type 3 accessible rooms include a roll-in shower and they are the most accessible rooms on the property.

Accessible parking is located in front of room 202, with level access over to the room. Access features include wide doorways, a lowered peephole and good pathway access. It's furnished with two 25-inch high queen-sized beds with access on all sides, a table with a chair, a chest of drawers and a refrigerator.

The spacious bathroom is equipped with a roll-in shower with grab bars, a hand-held showerhead and a fold-down shower bench. The toilet has a grab bar on the back wall, and offers wheelchair access on both sides. The bathroom also includes a roll-under sink.

Room 208 is also a classic cottage with Type 3 accessibility features. It includes the same access features and bedroom furnishings as room 202. The bathroom is equipped with a roll-in shower with grab bars, a hand-held showerhead and a fold-down shower seat. It also has a roll-under sink; however the toilet grab bars in this unit are located on the back and right walls (as seated).

A portable shower chair and step stool (for the beds) are available for these — or any — rooms at Jackson Lake Lodge. Additionally, the property operates a free accessible shuttle to take guests between the main lodge and their rooms. Luggage delivery service is also available. In short, the staff does everything they can to ensure guests a comfortable stay.

There's good access to all of the public areas — which are located on the second floor of the main lodge — at this property too. There's elevator access from the first floor to the comfortable second-floor lobby, which features floor-to-ceiling windows that offer stunning mountain views. Two massive fireplaces occupy the opposite corners of the lobby, with comfortable seating in between. There's barrier-free access to the Mural Room Restaurant, the Pioneer Grill and the Blue Heron Lounge, which are located off the lobby; and good pathway access to the coffee kiosk in the center. It's a beautiful, functional and accessible public space.

Jackson Lake Lodge is open from mid-May to early October.

Colter Bay Village Cabins

100 Cabin Road
Moran, WY 83013
(307) 543-3100
www.gtlc.com

This lakeshore property is comprised of 166 lodgepole pine cabins scattered throughout the forest. Each cabin has its own history, as they were relocated from homesteads throughout the park when Colter Bay was developed. The building that makes up the guest lounge and the two accessible cabins once housed the guest lounge, dining room, kitchen and the office at the Square G Ranch, which was located on the old road to Leigh and Jenny Lakes. Even though this historic building dates back to the 1920s, access modifications have been added over the years to make it wheelchair-accessible today.

Accessible parking is located in front of the cabin office, which was also part of the Square G Ranch. Ramp access has been added, and even though there's a slight lip at the doorway it's doable with a little assistance. Inside there's plenty of room to navigate a wheelchair, and barrier-free access over to the registration desk.

The accessible cabins are located a short drive away, in the heart of the complex. Accessible parking is located in front of cabin 456, with a

Cabin 458 at Colter Bay Village Cabins

Interior of cabin 458 at Colter Bay Village Cabins

level pathway over to the front door. Inside there's good pathway access throughout the unit, which has wood floors for easy rolling. The cabin is furnished with two 25-inch high double beds and one 25-inch high twin bed. The beds, which are located in different corners of the room, each have wheelchair access on one side.

The bathroom has a wide doorway and a full five-foot turning radius. It's equipped with a roll-in shower with grab bars and a hand-held showerhead. Even though there's a slight one-inch lip on the shower, it's still possible to

Bathroom in cabin 458 at Colter Bay Village Cabins

easily transfer to the fold-down shower bench because of the extra space in the bathroom. The toilet grab bars are located on the back and left walls (as seated), and the bathroom also has a roll-under sink.

Cabin 458 is located just around the corner. This spacious unit, which was described as "large enough to be a bridal suite" by the front desk clerk, is twice the size of cabin 456. That said, since these cabins have the same bed configuration and are in the same rate category they rent for the same price.

Cabin 458 also has accessible parking in front, with a paved path over to the front door. Inside, there's room enough to maneuver even the largest wheelchair or scooter, around the furnishings. There's wheelchair access on the right side of the twin and one double bed (as you face them), and on both sides of the other double bed. And as in cabin 456. all of the beds are 25 inches high. Other furnishings include a sofa, a chair, and a desk with a chair.

The bathroom has the exact same access features as cabin 456. Additionally there's a walk-in closet that's large enough to be a room, located directly across from the bathroom. This spacious unit is especially suited for people with large wheelchairs or scooters, or for those traveling with an attendant.

There's also level access to the large guest lounge, located between the accessible cabins. There's plenty of room to roll around the tables, chairs and sofas, and it's technically the only place on the property that has free Wi-Fi. I say "technically" because you can also get good reception in the adjacent accessible cabins because of their proximity to the source.

This historic property, which was developed as an affordable family lodging choice, makes a great accessible home base for any Grand Teton stay.

This property is open from late May to late September.

Signal Mountain Lodge

1 Inner Park Road
Moran, WY 83013
(307) 543-2831
www.signalmountainlodge.com

Located on the east shore of Jackson Lake, Signal Mountain Lodge dates back to the 1920s, when the property was a go-to choice for wealthy outdoorsmen. Historic log cabins still dot the parcel, and a nice variety of bungalows, cabins, country rooms and secluded retreats are scattered through the lakeside forest near the main lodge complex. Over the years upgrades and modifications have been made to Signal Mountain Lodge, and today this 79-unit property offers two nicely accessible lake view cabins, both of which have roll-in showers.

There's an accessible drop-off area in front of the main lodge building, with ramp access to the front door. Inside there's plenty of room to maneuver a wheelchair around the lobby, which offers an expansive lake view. There's also barrier-free access over to the registration desk, and to the accessible restrooms, which are located near the front door.

Cabin 130 is located a short drive from the main lodge building, and it features accessible parking and ramp access up to the front porch. There's

Jackson Lake viewed from cabins 128 and 130 at Signal Mountain Lodge

Interior of cabin 130 at Signal Mountain Lodge

a nice view of Jackson Lake from the front porch, and plenty of room to maneuver a wheelchair out there. Cabin access features include wide doorways, a lowered peephole and excellent pathway access throughout the unit.

The log cabin is furnished with two 26-inch high queen-sized beds with an access aisle between them, a bedside table, a chest of drawers, a microwave and a refrigerator. There's also a small dining table with four chairs over by the window — again with a nice lake view.

Bathroom in cabin 130 at Signal Mountain Lodge

The bathroom has a full five-foot turning radius and it's equipped with a roll-in shower with grab bars and a hand-held showerhead. There's also a standard showerhead in the enclosure. The toilet grab bars are located on the back and right walls (as seated), and the bathroom also has a roll-under sink and a portable shower chair. Top it off with a lowered full-length mirror — an often overlooked feature — and you have a comfortable accessible cabin.

Cabin 128, which is located next door, has the same access features as cabin 130.

The bulk of the public areas, including the Peaks Restaurant, Deadman's Bar and the Trapper Grill, are located in a large building between the gas station and the main lodge building. There's accessible parking near the front door, and barrier-free access to all inside areas, including the accessible restrooms.

In short they did an excellent job of access at this historic mountain property, and that's something you just don't see every day.

Signal Mountain Lodge is open from early May through mid-October.

Parking for Cabins 128 and 130 at Signal Mountain Lodge

Access Overview

Grand Teton National Park offers a number of scenic drives, with panoramic windshield views and accessible overlooks and viewpoints along the routes. Some of the top choices include the popular Jenny Lake Scenic Drive, as well as routes along Teton Park Drive, Highway 191 and Signal Mountain Summit Road. Additionally, thanks to the $19 million Jenny Lake Renewal Project, a half-mile accessible trail now skirts the lakeshore. Add in a gaggle of accessible trails and almost 10 miles of accessible multiuse paths, and there's no shortage of activities for wheelchair-users and slow walkers. That said, take it slow and remember to hydrate, as the average altitude along the main park roads is 6,800 feet.

Jenny Lake is one of the more poplar areas of the park. and besides the new accessible trail, wheelchair-users and slow walkers can also enjoy a one-hour cruise courtesy of Jenny Lake Boating. There's level access to the dock, which is located a short walk from the Jenny Lake Visitor Center; and ramp access to the boats. All of the boats are accessible, and they each have four sets of tie-downs; although most people opt not to use them on the calm waters of Jenny Lake.

An eight-mile section of the multiuse trail also runs from Jenny Lake to the park entrance, with accessible stops at Teton Glacier Turnout, Cottonwood

Dock at Jenny Lake

Creek Picnic Area, Windy Point Turnout, Taggart Lake Trailhead, and the Craig Thomas Discovery and Visitor Center. This paved trail is wide, mostly level and is an excellent choice for wheelers, walkers and handcyclists. A 1.25-mile spur also runs from Moose Junction to Antelope Flats along the Highway 191 corridor, with an access point in the Blacktail Butte Trailhead parking area, near Antelope Flats Road.

There's also a paved level trail along the east shore of Jackson Lake. From the Colter Bay Visitor Center, the trails leads .3-miles north to the amphitheater, then follows the lakeshore for another .3-miles. The wide level trail has a few bumps in the pavement but they are easy to dodge; and along the way you'll be treated to some picture-perfect lake views.

There's another accessible trail over at Jackson Lake Dam, but it's a little hard to find. Just follow the signs to the restrooms and park as close to the vault toilet as possible. The accessible path to a nice .2-mile accessible trail along the reservoir is located next to the vault toilet; and it should be noted that this is the only accessible way to get to the dam. The sidewalk from the lower parking area is too steep — and too dangerous — for wheelchairs. The accessible trail, which is mostly paved, winds along the shore, and offers a few interpretive plaques and benches along the way. The trail ends at Teton Park Road, where you can make a left on the level sidewalk and walk out over the dam for about .1 mile.

Accessible trail at Jackson Lake Dam

Menor's Ferry Historic District, which dates back to 1894, is also worth a stop. A .3-mile trail passes the old general store, the ferry and the blacksmith's shop before it reaches the Maud Noble Cabin, where plans were first made to make Grand Teton a national park back in 1923. After that, the trail crosses a field and loops back to the parking lot. It's a pleasant level walk, with lots to see along the way.

Finally, make sure and stop at the most iconic structure in the park — the historic T. A Moulton Barn — which is located off Antelope Flats Road in the Mormon Row Historic District. Just turn south on Mormon Row, and park in the semi-paved unstriped parking area near the accessible vault toilet. The barn, which has adorned many a calendar, is located across from the parking area. Even if you can't walk far, you, can still enjoy this historic wooden structure framed by the towering Tetons. There's also a .3-mile hard-packed dirt trail that leads from the parking area down to the Andrew & Ida Chambers homestead, which features a gaggle or old barns and corrals.

Don't Miss This

Most visitors flock to the well publicized Jenny Lake Trail, and completely miss the equally accessible String Lake Trail. This mostly-paved accessible trail winds along the lakeshore, and offers a good taste of the flora and fauna

Historic T. A. Moulton Barn in the Mormon Row Historic District

Bench along the trail at String Lake

that frequent this glacial lake. It can be accessed from either of the two parking lots located along String Lake Road, near Jenny Lake Lodge. The first lot is close to the accessible canoe launch, and the second one is near a picnic area. The half-mile trail is sheltered by a forest, and includes a bench or two along the route; and the whole circuit makes for a nice one-mile round-trip hike. Pack along a picnic lunch and enjoy a post-hike repast.

Insider Tip

Most visitors drive right on by an off-the-beaten-path accessible trail along the Jenny Lake Scenic Drive, mostly because it's not noted on any of the park maps. It's located near the end of the route — just look for an accessible parking space on the right. A wide paved service road, located next to the parking space, winds through the forest and leads to the campground, where you can make a right and follow an accessible .16 mile path to the ranger station. From there you can connect to the accessible portion of the Jenny Lake Trail which follows the lakeshore. As an added bonus, there's not much traffic along this route, because it's relatively unknown.

Resources

Grand Teton National Park
(307) 739-3399
www.nps.gov/grte
www.facebook.com/GrandTetonNPS
twitter.com/GrandTetonNPS

Road Conditions
(307) 739-3682

Jenny Lake Cruise & Shuttle
(307) 734-9227
www.jennylakeboating.com

Grand Teton Lodge Company (NPS Concessionaire)
(307) 543-3100
www.gtlc.com
www.facebook.com/grandtetonlodgeco
twitter.com/tetontales
Jenny Lake Lodge
Jackson Lake Lodge
Colter Bay Village Cabins

Forever Resorts (NPS Concessionaire)
(307) 543-2831
www.signalmountainlodge.com
www.facebook.com/Signal.Mountain.Lodge
Signal Mountain Lodge

Barrier-Free Travel; Glacier, Yellowstone and Grand Teton National Parks for Wheelers and Slow Walkers
www.barrierfreeyellowstone.com

Access Resources

Emerging Horizons

www.EmergingHorizons.com
Your one-stop accessible travel resource.

- Destinations
- Lodging Options
- Tour Companies
- Travel News
- Trails & Recreation
- Travel Tips

Barrier-Free National Parks

www.barrierfreenationalparks.com
Access information on some of America's top national parks.

- Insider Tips
- Resources
- Suggested Itineraries
- Access Photos

Barrier-Free Travel
Yosemite, Sequoia and Kings Canyon National Parks
for Wheelers and Slow Walkers

By Candy B. Harrington

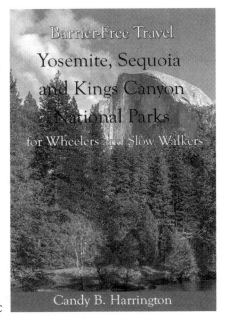

This indisputable guidebook includes detailed access information that will help wheelchair-users and slow walkers find an accessible room and build a barrier-free itinerary in Central California's top three national parks. Along with updated information about accessible trails, boardwalks, viewpoints, museums and picnic areas, this helpful resource also includes detailed access evaluations and photographs of 33 properties in and near the parks. And if you'd like to sleep under the stars, barrier-free campsites are also noted. Add in helpful details about the location of local airports, and the availability of accessible shuttles, public transportation and van rentals, and you've got all the information you need to get to and around the parks. Top it off with information on accessible bus tours, ranger programs, wheelchair and handcycle rentals and you have a must-have resource for wheelchair-users, stroller parents or anybody who just needs to take things a little slower.

www.barrierfreeyosemite.com

Barrier-Free Travel
Glacier, Yellowstone and Grand Teton National Parks
for Wheelers and Slow Walkers

By Candy B. Harrington

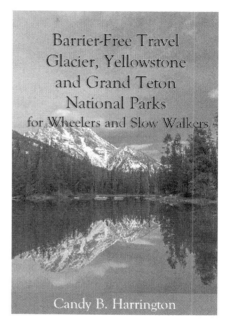

Penned by accessible travel expert Candy B. Harrington, this access guide includes detailed information about accessible trails, picnic areas, lodging options and attractions in Glacier, Yellowstone and Grand Teton National Parks. This handy resource features access details and photos of over 40 lodging options, including all in-park lodgings, as well as gateway city offerings. Details on accessible bus and boat tours, and shuttle service to, from and in the parks are also included. Top it off with information on recent access upgrades, barrier-free camping, and Amtrak, airport and accessible van rental details, and you have a one-stop national park resource. This guide will help you find an accessible room that works for you, and plan a accessible itinerary based on your abilities, to these three favorite national parks.

www.barrierfreeyellowstone.com

Barrier-Free Travel
The Grand Canyon
for Wheelers and Slow Walkers

By Candy B. Harrington

Penned by accessible travel expert
Candy B. Harrington, this guidebook
offers hard-to-find access information
that will help wheelchair-users and
slow walkers plan the ultimate road
trip to Grand Canyon National Park.
It offers detailed access information
about trails and attractions in Grand
Canyon National Park, as well as access
details about lodging and attractions
in gateway cities and Grand Canyon
West. Accessible lodging choices,
restaurants and attractions along
Arizona's Interstate 40 and Route
66 are also noted. Information on
accessible transfers from area airports
and Amtrak stations, and details
about nearby accessible van rentals are

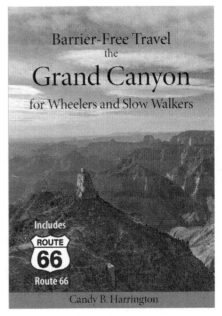

included. A must-read if the Grand Canyon is on your bucket list.

www.barrierfreegrandcanyon.com